"Mandy Smith's *Unfettered* helps us discard our Westernized baggage so we can be formed all over again as children in awe of God. With lively prose and a profound wisdom, she teaches us how to dance with God. Open these pages and allow yourself to be drawn in to this childlike way of life with God. Learn the postures of resting, receiving, and responding. Explore knowing God."

—**David Fitch**, professor, Northern Seminary; author of *Faithful Presence*

"Few writers are able to combine cultural criticism and hopeful imagination for the future in the manner that Mandy Smith does. *Unfettered* is essential reading, a wise guide to tiptoeing into a vibrant, post-Christendom faith. It is a much-needed book, and at the same time a dangerous one, for one cannot read it and remain unchanged."

—**C. Christopher Smith**, founding editor of *The Englewood Review of Books*; author of *How the Body of Christ Talks*

"This rare book on childlikeness is written by someone who is herself charmingly childlike in her approach to God, people, and the world. Mandy is a well-informed writer, and she is also a profoundly enchanting one as she pens what could prove to be the manifesto for the always-possible, ever-resurgent, Order of the Eternal Child. Viva!"

—**Alan Hirsch**, founder of Forge Missional Training Network and the Movement Leaders Collective; author of *The Forgotten Ways*

"When it comes to getting at the core of the problem of the fractured self, Smith strikes at the heart of the dualism of Western culture with her analysis in *Unfettered*. Unwavering in her commitment to unravel the quandary that Christianity in the West has trapped itself in and unflinching in her determination to tell the narrative of one who would gather all creation into wholeness, Smith makes a clear case for seeing with renewed eyes and hearing with unclogged ears. *Unfettered* provides space for reflection where we can find our full humanity and abandon the need to 'fix' our lives. It is an invitation to lean into the uncomfortable void and therefore create room where we can exist, grow, and flourish."

—**Phuc Luu**, author of *Jesus of the East: Reclaiming the Gospel for the Wounded*

"We have pastor-practitioners and pastor-scholars, but we need pastor-artists because they help us encounter God as Mystery. Mandy Smith is a pastor-artist. In *Unfettered*, Mandy invites us to dance a three-step of rest, receive, and respond. She shows us what we can be: human beings deeply connected to God, self, and others. Mandy doesn't make it sound easy; she just makes it sound so very worth it. She invites us to a dance that lives fully into the goodness of God. I've been grateful for Mandy's voice for a long time now, and *Unfettered* is an overdue guide for those of us wanting another way."

—**Steve Cuss**, lead pastor of Discovery Christian Church, Broomfield, Colorado

"Being quite skilled at the controlling, adultish ways of exegeting Scripture, I was deeply confronted by Mandy Smith's rest-receive-respond approach. She invites us to divest ourselves of our need to be masters of the text and, like children, allow our senses, our instincts, even our bodies, to contribute to hearing from God. Like Nicodemus asking Jesus how one becomes born again, I found myself regularly resisting, questioning, and doubting Mandy's new method before being won over by her approach. If you want to contend with the Good News in your heart, mind, and body, read this book!"

—**Michael Frost**, Morling College, Sydney

Unfettered

Imagining a Childlike Faith
beyond the Baggage of Western Culture

Mandy Smith

Foreword by
Walter Brueggemann

Brazos Press
a division of Baker Publishing Group
Grand Rapids, Michigan

For Vera

© 2021 by Mandy Smith

Published by Brazos Press
a division of Baker Publishing Group
PO Box 6287, Grand Rapids, MI 49516-6287
www.brazospress.com

Printed in the United States of America

All rights reserved. No part of this publication may be reproduced, stored in a retrieval system, or transmitted in any form or by any means—for example, electronic, photocopy, recording—without the prior written permission of the publisher. The only exception is brief quotations in printed reviews.

Library of Congress Cataloging-in-Publication Data
Names: Smith, Mandy, 1971– author.
Title: Unfettered : imagining a childlike faith beyond the baggage of Western culture / Mandy Smith ; foreword by Walter Brueggemann.
Description: Grand Rapids, Michigan : Brazos Press, a division of Baker Publishing Group, [2021]
Identifiers: LCCN 2020042367 | ISBN 9781587435058 (paperback) | ISBN 9781587435324 (casebound)
Subjects: LCSH: Christianity and culture.
Classification: LCC BR115.C8 S58385 2021 | DDC 261—dc23
LC record available at https://lccn.loc.gov/2020042367

Unless otherwise indicated, Scripture quotations are from THE HOLY BIBLE, NEW INTERNATIONAL VERSION®, NIV® Copyright © 1973, 1978, 1984, 2011 by Biblica, Inc.® Used by permission. All rights reserved worldwide.

Scripture quotations labeled NRSV are from the New Revised Standard Version of the Bible, copyright © 1989 National Council of the Churches of Christ in the United States of America. Used by permission. All rights reserved.

21 22 23 24 25 26 27   7 6 5 4 3 2 1

In keeping with biblical principles of creation stewardship, Baker Publishing Group advocates the responsible use of our natural resources. As a member of the Green Press Initiative, our company uses recycled paper when possible. The text paper of this book is composed in part of post-consumer waste.

Contents

Foreword

Walter Brueggemann

Do not, dear reader, take up this book unless you intend to be changed, because this book concerns emancipatory transformation. In poetic idiom, Mandy Smith has written a narrative account of her wondrous awakening to the gifts of freedom and grace in her life that have taken her by surprise. Her quite personal account is intended as an invitation and a summons to her readers that they, like the author, might come to live differently in the world.

Smith names and effectively resists "empire," a stand-in for the seductions of modernity that vie for control, certitude, and predictability. It is clear that this mode of life cannot deliver on our hopes for humanness. Smith has seen that in her own life, her previous practice of faith seduced her into certitude and control that denied her the freedom, joy, and grace to which such "imperial" faith often attested. She found that her imagination had been occupied by and limited to the rigidities of orthodoxy that had become the very enemy of that which it advocated.

Smith is a compelling storyteller. The pivotal story she tells is about the life-changing moment when, during her sabbatical, she observed a flock of flying geese. She saw that without a plan the geese readily formed the shape of a V in the sky: "The shoulders of a goose know how to find the space where the wind is kind. And without conscious effort they are flying in a perfect V." As she observed this oft-reenacted wonder, Smith resolved, "I want to fly like that." This book is about her flight lessons and her newly acquired capacity to soar. Her poetic gifts not only bear witness to that new joyous freedom but also invite her readers to take flight.

Another gripping tale she tells is about how the night before a daring meeting to be convened for prayers of healing (which struck her as awkward and a bit embarrassing), she went alone to the church sanctuary to act out her uneasiness about the enterprise. There, alone in the sanctuary, she danced in anticipation and protest and demand:

> My shoulder stiffly twitched, as I clenched my eyes shut to avoid witnessing my own awkwardness. I don't know what it looked like, but I danced. I pictured the faces of those we would pray over in the morning, and I danced for each one. I felt my muscles begin to loosen, my heart open a crack, my longing leak out, and a little joy shyly emerge. By the end, I was sweating, not because my dance was so exuberant but from the exertion of will it took to override my lament, dancing when I felt like weeping. Psalm 30 expresses it this way: "You turned my wailing into dancing; you removed my sackcloth and clothed me with joy" (v. 11).

At this point Smith was in a new world that was given to her, one that she had not anticipated or chosen. From her deep faith and restless readiness, she has been able to formulate a three-step movement into this new gift.

Rest. It is important that Smith's notice of the geese that "fly like that" was during her sabbatical, when she was taking a break from the pressures of empire. She knew then and knows now that without such restful attentiveness one is not likely to engage such emancipatory reality. This is a good, strong word for those of us who maintain "religious busyness" in our lives.

Receive. The empire requires us to keep taking initiatives—to manage, produce, and generate. But rest puts us in a posture to be on the receiving end of reality that does not start with us and therefore does not depend on us. In a posture of rest we might receive gifts that are being given by the goodness of God via the wonders of creation. Thus Smith, for the first time, began to pay attention to "the book of nature" that is as revelatory as "the book of Scripture."

She found all around her wonder, gift, and mystery that have turned out to be buoyant and sustaining. It is therefore not a surprise that Smith finds the mundane of creation to be Spirit-filled in its restorative gifts.

Respond. When we receive, we then can respond. The response to which Smith finds herself committed is a ministry of healing and reconciliation among her neighbors. That ministry in response, however, does not require (or permit) that we be self-starters. As a result, in this sequence of rest-receive-respond there is no risk of burnout or fatigue or excessive managerial burden because the response is enveloped in receptivity.

Smith's fresh awareness is that we may become "childlike" in awe, wonder, innocence, and trust. She observes that an excessive passion to be a knowing, responsible adult serves the empire of control, certitude, and predictability. She is, moreover, acutely aware of the oft-repeated warning that in becoming "childlike" we should not become "childish." But she knows very well that being childlike has nothing to do with being childish, so she tersely dismisses that warning. And then in what I think is a brilliant maneuver, she observes that in a parallel way being an adult runs the risk of making us "adultish"—that is, overly responsible and obsessed with making everything come out right. She sees that in the empire the risk of becoming adultish is even greater than the risk of being childish. So much for the empire of control!

Before I finish, I will comment on two terrific images Smith offers. First, she reports that she has learned that God is not some kind of "encyclopedia in the sky." Second, she reflects on her old desire to meet with God for a "business meeting" only to find that God had in mind a "picnic." What a trade-off! The picnic sounds like an echo of the wondrous affirmation of the Westminster Shorter Catechism that our chief end is to glorify God and enjoy God forever.

Smith's book is primarily addressed to her own circle of faith—namely, evangelicals who are too certain about all matters of faith. But I read as a "liberal Christian," and her book surely pertains as well to my circle of faith wherein liberals are filled with their own certitude and bottomless convictions about what is to be done. Indeed, liberal Christians readily assume that we are the real adults in the room. In a rejection of such certitude among evangelical and progressive Christians, Smith invites us all to rest in the Spirit. Smith "could have danced all night" and nearly did. It was a dance of tears that turned to joy. Smith knows that when we are preoccupied with presiding over God's "business meeting," we may miss the dance of the Spirit. This book is a powerfully compelling good word to the church in our society—evangelical and liberal—that has largely exhausted its old endowments. Isaiah 40:31 exhorts us to "soar on wings like eagles," to "run and not grow weary," and to "walk and not be faint."

Fly like that!

Acknowledgments

This book may have my name on the cover, but it is the expression of many rich conversations and community adventures.

Thank you, Bob Hosack and all at Brazos, for your adventurous spirits, and to Karen Swallow Prior for introducing us.

Thank you to all who have affirmed the call to "Fly like that": Justin Dunn, Jared Siebert, Cyd and Geoff Holsclaw, Kathy Callahan-Howell, Sandie Brock, Stephanie Young, Tiffany Mills, John and Kate Pattison, Susan Carson, Candyce Roberts, Deb and Al Hirsch, Steve and Liesl Huhn, MaryKate Morse, Cherith Fee Nordling, Ruth Anne Reese, Cheryl McCarthy, and all my friends at Ecclesia Network and Missio Alliance.

Thank you, Joshua Retterer, Scott Jones, Dave Hansen, Paul Pastor, and Sister Dorothy Schuette for telling me to write. And then telling me again.

Thank you to Meg and D. J. and Trischler Design Company for loaning me your imaginations and helping me remember why I'm doing this.

Thank you to everyone at Ben and Julia's wedding, All Things New Fest, and Nowhere Else Fest for being the first to dance with me (some metaphorically, some literally)!

Thank you to my UCC family—and to all my "guinea pigs" there—for showing me what it means to be lost and found in the body of Christ!

Thank you to Wendy and Mum and Dad: because of you it's not hard to imagine the kingdom as a loving family.

Thank you to Jamie, Zoë, Kieran, and Jathan. What a gift it is to figure out childlike-adultlikeness with you all!

For the Lord of Every Story: thank you that you didn't want to do this without us.

Introduction

The goal of knowing is not complete
information; it is communion.

—Esther Lightcap Meek,
A Little Manual for Knowledge

Our concern as followers of Jesus is neither
with a religion called "Christianity," nor with
a culture called "Western Civilization,"
but with a person, Jesus of Nazareth.

—John Stott, "In Christ,"
in *Knowing and Doing*

Western culture is in a tailspin, and Christian faith is entangled in it. Before we can begin the work of disentangling from Western culture, we first need to identify how we are shaped by it. We have inherited from our Western, Enlightenment, industrial culture certain ingrained ways of being that can be detrimental to our faith. These habits can be summed up in the phrases "I think, therefore I am" and "I do, therefore I am."

1

First, "I think, therefore I am," a phrase coined by René Descartes, sidelines emotions, instinct, nature, mystery, and bodily experience. When faith is mostly based on information, it leads to dryness and doubt. As James K. A. Smith puts it, "[The] (Protestant) church still tends to see us as Cartesian minds. While secular liturgies are after our hearts through our bodies, the church thinks it only has to get into our heads."[1]

Second, "I do, therefore I am" has not been as clearly articulated as Descartes's statement above, but Western culture is built on the assumption that human agency is the hope of the world. While this premise seems empowering, it actually leads to oppression, depression, anxiety, and burnout. It also leaves little room for partnership with God. Brennan Manning knows the desperate irony of this gospel of independence:

> The . . . church today accepts grace in theory but denies it in practice. . . . We believe that we can pull ourselves up by our bootstraps—indeed, we can do it ourselves. Sooner or later we are confronted with the painful truth of our inadequacy and insufficiency. Our security is shattered and our bootstraps are cut. . . . Our huffing and puffing to impress God, our scrambling for brownie points, our thrashing about trying to fix ourselves while hiding our pettiness and wallowing in guilt are nauseating to God and are a flat denial of the gospel of grace.[2]

FIELD GUIDE

How do you see these "I think, therefore I am" and "I do, therefore I am" realities at work in your own experience of faith, in your church, and in the church at large? What should we do about it?

If you're anything like me, your response to this summary of our situation would look something like this: "Oh, this is a problem! We should *think* of new ways to *fix* this!" We're stuck in these habits of thinking and self-sufficiency. I attend many gatherings of Christians where we sit and talk and lament and problem solve. We would say that theology is more than ideas and that the hope of the world is not all up to us. But when we spend all our time thinking and planning, our very habits make a theological statement. *How* we do things is theological. All of life is a confession of our doctrine. And not all the belief we claim with our habits and postures resonates with the belief we claim with our mouths. If we really believed that there is more to faith than ideas alone and that there are more ways forward than we could find in our own strength, how would we live and be the church?

Both of these habits—"I think, therefore I am" and "I do, therefore I am"—look more like Western culture than Christianity but have become foundational postures in the Western church. We do kingdom things in empire ways, which doesn't look like good news. The way forward cannot be found through our usual approach—new ideas we arrive at on our own. But we have been so steeped in this culture that we're oblivious to our own perpetuation of the problem, even as we try to troubleshoot the problem. This is going to take more than thinking differently. This is going to take detox. And detox is messy, especially if the thing we need to detox from is our own control.

I propose that a way forward can be found in Jesus's surprising invitation to the kingdom through childlikeness. Here's why:

1. Children identify and engage as whole (thinking, feeling, sensing, embodied, relational) selves.
2. Children know how to engage without taking on full responsibility.

Unashamed of Humanness

Here's where the incompatibility of Christianity and Western culture comes to a head: to be a Christian is to be like a child, someone incomplete and open to outside guidance, things that are anathema in the West. As Willem Vanderburg puts it, we "begin to understand why the Christian Bible insists on believers becoming like children. . . . Children . . . do not act as if their mental map is complete and reliable; they are open to outside guidance. Adults, on the other hand, choose to live as if their mental map is the final word on everything, and this makes it impossible for them to live any longer in the world with a certain playfulness as children do."[3] Western culture tells us we should be complete and independent. It tempts us to believe we can escape our ordinary, human limitations—weakness, sickness, incapacity, ignorance. We swim in water that is toxic to humans. The more we bring that toxic culture into our Christian practices, the more we strip our faith of every way God wants to redeem us as ordinary, limited humans.

As I write, I have just heard that my son's university is shutting down temporarily in response to the COVID-19 outbreak. And I have just been in conversation with local church leaders about whether we will be holding services this Sunday. In my lifetime I have never heard of a crisis as far-reaching as this one. Not only is it sparking fear about health but it is also frustrating our plans. The couple whose wedding and Italian honeymoon

FIELD GUIDE

Advertisements give us an interesting insight into our cultural values. Pay attention to the underlying messages of advertisements you see, how they subtly judge every way we feel ordinary human limitation.

were supposed to happen is out of luck. It is also affecting family businesses (If we're all staying home, how will the local café survive?), which in turn affects the global economy. And there's very little we can do about it. All our usual efforts to overcome problems have not been able to overcome this tiny virus that has shut down the planet. The simple steps of staying home and washing our hands are infuriating to people who are accustomed to solving problems and controlling things. We've come to the end of ourselves.

And when we do finally come to the end of ourselves, it's such a strange, new experience for Westerners that we feel like failures. Into that moment of failure our culture inserts its impatience for human limitation, offering us only two choices: fall into the anxiety of adultish hyperengagement (we'd better fix this) or into the despair of childish disengagement (we're beyond hope). For hyperengagement we're offered many remedies—every question has a search bar, every hunger has a product, every lackluster skill set has a conference. Every limited power has a quick-fix promise. This lifestyle works—until it doesn't. And for despair our culture offers us any number of dulling agents, which only deepen the disengagement. Everyone else seems strong and capable so we get wrapped up in a desperate cycle of hiding inadequacy from those who are desperately trying to hide their inadequacy from us. "The point then is to help break the false distinction between the idea that there are those who are whole and those who have a lack. For the true distinction is between those who hide their lack under the fiction of wholeness and those who are able to embrace it."[4]

We don't like confronting the ways we are small or inadequate. I'm not talking only about personal failings or weakness of character; we should always be open to personal growth and development. I'm talking here about the ways all humans are just that: human—never able to fix, control, understand everything. We run out of energy and ideas. We get tired, sick, and old. All the while quietly loathing ourselves for it. This fundamental reality of our own humanness makes us itch to escape our own skin.

And yet Jesus was willing to be human, more willing to be human than we are. As we are reminded in Hebrews 2:7, Jesus was made just a little lower than the angels. For a while, he was just like us, fully human in every way. He was willing to walk around on two feet, bringing the kingdom through his ordinary voice and hands. The wilderness temptations all made alluring promises that Jesus's mission could be achieved in a more spectacular, "superhuman" way. And he said no every time. He wasn't ashamed of humanness—his own or ours. I'm starting to think that we don't get what Jesus offers us because we can't bear his human ordinariness and frailty. Why would we want to see it in him when we can't acknowledge it in ourselves?

Hebrews 2 goes on to make a surprising claim: all things have been subjected to humans. God left nothing outside our control, but Scripture is quick to add that we don't see that yet (v. 8). Instead, we feel subjected to, overwhelmed with, dominated by all things. Forces of nature smash our cities, viruses make us housebound, weather thwarts our plans, tiredness interferes with our productivity—it's hard to imagine how all things have been made subject to us.

French Christian philosopher and activist Jacques Ellul anticipated how contemporary life and faith would evolve in a technological world, how we would be tempted to avoid—or at least defer—our not-enoughness. As he puts it,

> Before God I am a human being. . . . But I am caught in a situation from which there is truly and radically no escape, in a spider's web I cannot break. If I am to continue to be a living human being, someone must come to free me. In other words, God is not trying to humiliate me. What is mortally affronted in this situation is not my humanity or my dignity. It is my pride,

the vainglorious declaration that I can do it all myself. This we cannot accept. In our own eyes we have to declare ourselves to be righteous and free. We do not want grace. Fundamentally what we want is self-justification. There thus commences the patient work of reinterpreting revelation so as to make of it a Christianity that will glorify humanity and in which humanity will be able to take credit for its own righteousness.[5]

So out of our discomfort with our own humanness we have created a way of doing faith that has replaced a need for God with a human-made system of rules, beliefs, and traditions that makes us feel complete and self-sufficient. The technologies we employ to study God have allowed us to be our own saviors: we had the problem of limited understanding and we thought our own way out of it. If the only way to feel successful in our research of mystery is to kill the mystery, so be it! When our constant wrestling to get this right makes us feel foolish, we make a system, a list of rules, a doctrinal statement! Even if it just pushes our sense of failure down the track, at least we won't have to deal with it for now. What will it take to repent of an approach that landfills every lacuna? What will it take to finally acknowledge the human need God saw when he[6] entered the world as Jesus? How can we allow ourselves to once more experience whatever it is that God wants to save us from? Will we let him save us even from our ignorance of our need for a savior? As Simone Weil so beautifully puts it, "Grace fills empty spaces but it can only enter where there is a void to receive it, and it is grace itself which makes this void."[7]

Grace creates the void? Why would grace shape such a painful space? Why would a good God make us confront something so painful as what is lacking in ourselves? José Ortega y Gasset's analysis of Western culture presents a disturbingly hopeful possibility:

And this is the simple truth—that to live is to feel oneself lost—he who accepts it has already begun to find himself, to

7

be on firm ground. Instinctively, as do the shipwrecked, he will look round for something to which to cling, and that tragic, ruthless glance, absolutely sincere, because it is a question of his salvation, will cause him to bring order into the chaos of his life. These are the only genuine ideas; the ideas of the shipwrecked. All the rest is rhetoric, posturing, farce. He who does not really feel himself lost, is lost without remission; that is to say, he never finds himself, never comes up against his own reality.[8]

To live is to feel ourselves lost?! And hope is discovered in feeling ourselves hopeless?! As Western adults we assume that to be limited is to be shipwrecked, and that to be shipwrecked is to drown. But as children we felt small and it didn't cause existential crisis. We weren't surprised by life or our inability to control it, weren't ashamed of our need for something from outside of ourselves. In our awareness of and comfort with all that we weren't, we were free.

We've been good at these childlike habits before. We can find them again. As children we were able to engage in mystery with a spirit of adventure rather than of domination, joining with open hearts in something we didn't create. Detoxing from our addiction to domination seems impossible. Being unfettered from our bondage to cultural habits seems too much. Until we remember that before we were enmeshed with Western cultural habits, we lived and thrived. There are ways to return to those childlike habits, even in an adult life.

This is my story of the adventure of rediscovering the skills of adventure. An adventure is fun to read in a comfy armchair. But for those living the adventure, the thrill comes at great risk. So why would you take the risk to join this quest with me? This is where we see why testimony has been a big part of our tradition. When standing at the threshold of new adventure, our only reason to join may be the glint in the eyes of one who's come back to eagerly invite us in. This is why Anna Carter Florence proclaims, "Christian interpretation is not based in facts. It is based in testimony, which is an entirely different interpretive framework."[9]

The glint in my eye cannot be separated from the risk. I often wish we had a word for terrified-excited because that's where this adventure has taken me. And because I knew I was inviting readers to join me on something that felt risky, my first attempt to write came in the form of a thorough argument: four reasons why you should trust and join me. I hoped I could talk you into it. But there was no glint in my eye, there were no stories of how this adventure became revival in me, so I'm choosing instead to risk sharing the story—risky not only because it requires me to reveal my ordinary, subjective self but also because you may choose not to come with me. All I can say is that for the sake of the tiny glimpse of where this adventure is headed, I have been willing to lose everything, and those who have come with me have never looked back. I'm starting to understand why Jesus described the kingdom as a tiny treasure worth selling everything to gain. Will you join me as we discover it together? We may never be the same again!

While storytelling seems inconsequential, it can be powerful and transformative. Story stretches imaginations. Story speaks to both the left and the right brain, rewiring neural networks.[10] Story helps us empathize and feel less alone. And while it seems unrelated to the ways we're accustomed to doing theology, story provides rich language to describe the ways God reveals himself in human experience. As Stanley Hauerwas describes it, narrative theology is a "crucial conceptual category for such matters as understanding issues of epistemology and methods of argument, depicting personal identity, and displaying the content of Christian convictions."[11] A narrative approach to theology may seem, to some, like a contemporary fad, but "ancient writers understood that if believers were to remain faithful in the face of the strong currents pushing against faith, they would not only need strong arguments and clear explanations, they would also need those imaginative, emotional experiences that made their beliefs 'real.'"[12]

New Ways of Learning, New Ways of Seeing

Since old Western habits have, in the past, had us learning with only one part of ourselves and taking full responsibility for our learning, this new exploration will mean relearning how to learn even as we learn. The following pages tell my personal stories and describe the ways Scripture and various thinkers have been friends in the journey. What I share I share not as things I made but things I discovered, things we find already at work in the world when we learn how to listen and look. You're reading field notes of my adventure in forests and conversations and books and prayers. So I provide field guide moments throughout to invite you to also explore with all that you are. Together we can identify and engage as whole humans and do so knowing that insight is ours to receive as a gift, not wrestle from God by force. While personal experience (both mine and yours) may seem too ordinary to birth important things like theology, it's precisely because the study of God is so serious that we must take the risk to explore with all that we are. We may come to know with our whole selves and be known as whole selves. My prayer is that this adventure will help us to become unfettered from these deeply ingrained habits of Western culture so we know how to find and follow God with everything we are again and remember how to partner with him in his mission in the world.

If this way of learning is strange or uncomfortable for you, you are not alone. Unlike our usual habits of learning (read, research, then apply), this way of learning also felt backward to me. First, I explored, *then* read and researched to learn what others have discovered on this journey. It has helped me to discover that this seemingly backward approach has been described by theologian Don Browning. He compares our Western model of theological education (theory-to-practice model) with a more dynamic style of research: practice to theory and back to practice. "Practical thinking is the center of human thinking and . . . theoretical and technical thinking are abstractions from practical thinking. If one takes this seriously and relates it to theology, it fundamentally changes the historic formulations of the organization of theological disciplines. It is a revolution long overdue. . . . I argue that theology as a whole is fundamental practical theology."[13] This way of learning about God is less like reading an instruction manual and more like taking dancing lessons. My goal is not to shape a thorough argument but to share enough of my experience to invite you to join in too. I hope it opens more questions and possibilities than I can ever cover in one book. I hope it keeps you exploring with everything you have, everything you are, for the rest of your days.

Something about the way we've been studying God has been flawed. In our efforts to know him from a safe distance we've come up with findings that are lacking—perhaps not entirely wrong, but incomplete. Western Christian study of God has largely looked like the work of lab technicians. We capture glimpses of this wild God and wrest them from their natural habitat into a sterile environment where we can slice them into

"Christian theology has lost its way because it has neglected its purpose. . . . The flourishing of human beings and all God's creatures . . . is God's foremost concern for creation and should therefore be the central purpose of theology. . . . In an important sense, all Christians are theologians."

Miroslav Volf and Matthew Croasmun,
For the Life of the World: Theology That Makes a Difference

tiny specimens. When we're done, we seal them up in little jars with little labels, satisfied with our tidy taxonomy, even if something had to die in the process. While this kind of lab work is essential in actual scientific research, it's not the only way scientists study creatures. Fieldwork is also an essential part of scientific endeavors, and it's an approach we've neglected in our Western study of God. It's time to pull on our galoshes and to venture into this unsettling, vulnerable, wonderful way of doing theology.

Here's how this exploration will unfold: Chapter 1 invites a new posture—from the comfort of controlling our experience to one that rests from control. This endeavor to know a living, active thing means we must be willing to enter into its natural habitat, wait patiently for the moment it chooses to reveal itself, and be ready for the chase. It will mean naming how very daunting it is to enter the domain of a wild thing, how very risky it feels to wait for something that may or may not appear, how very humbling it is to know that we can't force the encounter, and how very exhilarating it is when something we did not create reveals itself. As children we were good at joining something we didn't initiate. We can do it again.

But our old Western habits run deep, and when we set them aside many hesitations will reveal themselves, as we'll explore in chapter 2. As we take the risk to rest from control and quietly wait for our wild God to reveal himself in his own way and time, those old habits will rise up in us: "This is a waste of time! There are more productive things I could be doing! What if it doesn't go as planned? What if I'm disappointed? What if I look foolish?" We'll have an opportunity to confront the false, adultish, hyperproductive mindset Western culture has shaped in us.

As we learn to set aside those very real Western fears, we'll discover that this childlike resting from our own control invites something remarkable! The more we've learned to watch and wait, the more we discover something we didn't expect, something all the more beautiful because it came as a gift! It may not be what we'd hoped for, but it may be what we need—a new way of seeing, an uncanny peace, a surprising prompt. Chapter 3 will help us trust and receive those unexpected gifts that arrive when we rest from control. Once we've overcome our hesitations and set aside control, there's always a surprising wisdom and power available to us. Chapter 4 doesn't need long to make this simple declaration: if we're resting, we always receive something, even if it's not what we'd planned.

Suddenly we find this thing we've only known in two dimensions is moving and breathing right in front of us, more terrifying and beautiful than we could have ever imagined! A thriving kingdom! A living God! The curiosity that drew us to study in the first place is still there, and now new parts of ourselves are awakened. Our ears pick up new frequencies, our hearts pound, our feet ache to follow. We are struck with an awareness of both how little we know and how much we love what we don't yet know. Now that we've rested enough to discover what's been waiting beyond our own self-sufficiency, we're invited to respond, to follow. Chapter 5 describes the ways we're asked to say yes to those invitations—to speak, act, give. What will it cost us to follow this living God, to discover this thriving kingdom, even with little understanding of where it's leading? Chapter 6 helps us work through new hesitations here, this time overcoming childish passivity and stepping into adultlike agency, embracing the possibility that we have something to contribute, small though it may seem.

All of this exploring the kingdom with our whole selves makes us wonder: "Is this legitimate? Is this scriptural? How do I understand this in light of how I've been taught the gospel?" So chapter 7 revisits Jesus's invitation into the kingdom through childlikeness, providing refreshing ways of understanding theology drawn from Scripture and Christian history. After following God with our whole selves and watching Scripture at work in the world, our dry Western ways of describing salvation will no longer do. We'll explore metaphors that are ancient and scriptural and more whole than our old Western habits of "I think, therefore I am" and "I do, therefore I am." We may come to know a gospel that lives and breathes with our daily joys and pains.

Finally, chapter 8 sums up this "Rest, Receive, Respond" way of life. It's a remedy for the false choice of "It's all up to God" or "It's all up to me." It's a life of daily partnership with the God of the universe who is already at work in the world. It's a way to be small without shame and powerful without oppressing. It's a way to trust that God will initiate the adventure and invite us every day to join him in it. It's a way to experience real, good news here and now in our hearts, minds, and bodies.

Since a book has limitations in inviting us into an embodied adventure, I'm offering additional materials, including a playlist with the songs that formed in me these lessons and online resources at www.UnfetteredBook.org/unfettered. Here you'll find blogposts, music and videos of practices and prayers, silences and silliness. I hope these add some fun and friendship for the journey.

Along the way we will discover that God already knows our human limitations. He knows all that makes us frail and curious and embodied and messy and glorious! The more we become comfortable (as God is) with our senses and instincts, our hearts and bodies—our very selves—as we were as children, the more we will discover the God who loves and rescues humans. We will remember how to be human like Jesus. As we do, we will confront how often our culture (unlike Jesus) shames humanness. And we will have many opportunities to finally be unfettered from the restraints of Western culture.

I begin all this simply with the story of a day I caught a glimpse of God in the wild and chose to take up the chase. Over the years since that day, this chase has taken me into oceans and libraries, dancing and tears, introspection and conversation, silence and singing, confusion and pain . . . and life. All that began in God's natural habitat of an ordinary day and an ordinary human heart. So let's begin there.

▶ A Soundtrack for Reading

Listen at www.UnfetteredBook.org/unfettered

Chapter 1: "I Will Go Plant Little Flowers" by Timbre

Chapter 2: "Gonna Let My Soul Catch My Body" by Over the Rhine

Chapter 3: "Holy, Holy, Holy" by Sufjan Stevens

Chapter 4: "Purge Me" by Urban Doxology

Chapter 5: "White Owl" by Josh Garrels*

Chapter 6: "The Mantis and the Moon" by Son of Laughter

  "Already Home" by Strahan

  "Romero" by The Project

  "Miserere" by Gregorio Allegri

  "The Wind May Be Beautiful" by Timbre

Chapter 7: "Viridissima" (from Hildegard von Bingen) by Jocelyn Montgomery and David Lynch

  "Song of the Sun" by Timbre

Chapter 8: "Butterfly" by Josh Garrells and Latifah Alattas

  "Jesus, Savior, Pilot Me" by Bifrost Arts and Laura Gibson

  "Encore un peu de temps – Vigiles" by the monks of Keur Moussa

  "The Kingdom of God" by Taizé

---

* Another selection for chapter 5, not included in the playlist, is "Unless the Seed Falls" by Tom Wuest, available at https://tomwuest.bandcamp.com/track/unless-the-seed-falls.

CHAPTER 1

Rest

Attention is the beginning of devotion.

—Mary Oliver, *Upstream*

With information we are alone;
in appreciation we are with all things.

—Abraham Heschel,
Man Is Not Alone

God does big things.
To us they seem very small.

I'm learning not to despise the day of small things.

My first day of small things was a Tuesday. I was on my first sabbatical. Although I was supposed to be resting, it is hard to break the habit of having an agenda. I knew from experience that reflection often leads to resolution. So without realizing it, my approach to God was, "Well, now that I have your attention, here's my list of problems for you to solve." But God seemed to have other plans. I wanted a business meeting; God wanted a picnic. His boredom with my questions soon became apparent, so I reluctantly joined the picnic. And while I didn't return to work with answers, I came back with a deeper knowledge that the Source of all Truth was present in a way I hadn't yet known.

If I'm honest, the offer of direct access to Truth the Person was a little deflating. Too nebulous for my taste. I'd rather just be given a set of rules, a system, a formula, an answer, direct access to an encyclopedia in the sky. Truth in the form of subject, verb, object. We don't usually want to be like Pharisees. But we all want to *feel* like Pharisees—standing on solid statements, having a place from which to argue. Given the choice between knowledge and life we prefer knowledge. It's how Adam and Eve chose their fruit. We've been choosing the same fruit ever since.

But I'm getting ahead of myself. My first day of small things took place a week into my pastoral sabbatical—a radical eight weeks of nothing in a world running on everything. I was on my usual morning walk—a daily practice of taking the cap off my overfull heart and mind so the contents could tumble out before God's kind eyes. What emerged on this particular March morning was obsessive wrangling with a troublesome situation that refused to be resolved. For the thousandth time I turned it over, willing it to take a more pleasing shape within my thinking so I could finally file it away. If this issue would just conform to my will I could have the resolution I needed to enjoy this sabbatical. Something on the edge of my awareness drew me outside my own head just in time to spot a flock of geese over the treetops. Their wings beat a breath across all my mental spreadsheets, a breath that made my heart sigh, "I want to fly like that."

Long after they were gone I stood there, breathless from the sudden change in me. For the first time I was aware that geese in formation have no plan to shape a V. Each goose doesn't measure two inches between its beak and the tail of the goose in front; instead, each goose attends to the art of sensing that slipstream sweet spot. The shoulders of a goose know how to find the space where the wind is kind. And without conscious effort they are flying in a perfect V—a perfect V for a human to behold from beneath on a Tuesday morning. A perfect V to draw her out of her efforts of measuring the inches in front of her own nose in her own desperate efforts at V-making. On that morning my "I want to fly like that" heart sigh became a sea change. I had no idea yet how to fly like that, but I had a feeling it would involve trusting parts of myself I'd ignored for a very long time. I had no idea what I was awakening or how often trusting those instincts would make me feel exactly like a goose in the worst possible way. I couldn't know then what it might grant me or cost me, but I've never forgotten my promise to fly differently. And I've never been the same.

I first understood this "I want to fly like that" promise as a nice project for an eight-week sabbatical. Nothing else to do, might as well learn to fly like a goose. On a warm Sunday morning soon after that first goose moment, my family dropped me off at a nearby park while they went on to church without me. In case I'd forgotten my previous promise, a very unsubtle second flock of geese swooped right over my head, reminding me to pay attention to any goose-like instincts that might make themselves known. I was halfway along a particularly long stretch of fence when I realized the fence needed a stick

FIELD GUIDE

What excites you about this invitation to "fly like that"? What makes you hesitate?

dragged along it. The sensible part of me did what it always did—dismissed the prompt as pointless and kept on walking. But the prompt persisted, and so my instinctive self marched my sensible self all the way back to the beginning of that fence to find a stick and begin again, this time to the sound of joyful clacking. I became self-conscious as a stranger passed me, and I wanted to cry, "Can't you see I'm learning to fly like a goose?! I'm going to drag this stick along this whole fence if it kills me!"

That night I wrote in my journal: "Maybe flying like a goose is about remembering your child self, wearing what you like, resting when you need, being sensitive to your body, and letting yourself follow your senses."[1] Learning whimsy for eight weeks was a great place to begin. I had no idea that it was just the beginning. Children's whims sometimes wander into significant things.

Trying to fly like a goose is strange when you don't have wings. But the metaphor became less strange as I remembered that this had once been my natural process. As children we trust our bodies and senses and emotions as much as we trust our thoughts. It helped to know that I wasn't learning a new skill but paying attention to parts of me that I had long disregarded. That childlike inclination, once awakened, began to make herself heard more and more. And my arguing with her became less and less heartfelt.

Rest from Running the World

This new permission to listen to childlike instincts was sealed in me by a man I expected to be deeply serious. At the start of a weeklong retreat at Gethsemani Abbey, the orientation talk was given by one of the most winsome, fully human beings I'd met. This eighty-year-old monk, recently come from a day of silence and prayer, embodied the possibility that profound spirituality and childlikeness were not only oddly compatible but symbiotic. His welcome invited me to sink into the rhythm of this place, and as I did I had a strangely familiar feeling. The monks prepare all meals for retreatants and ring the church bells when it's time for prayer. There was nothing I had to do, nowhere I had to be, no clock I had to watch. Since the retreat house is built into the side of their airy church sanctuary, I almost felt like the boy Samuel living in the temple. At any time I could cross the hallway from my simple room to an ordinary door that opened onto an extraordinary church space, filled somehow with a different kind of air. One night when I couldn't sleep, I heard the bells signaling for Vigils prayer at 3:15 a.m. I took my sleepy self down the hallway to join the monks, already dressed, already prepared for the day. Someone else was up, caring for the sleeping world, and it was just my part to show up and join the prayer, even if still in socked feet. It took me back to childhood mornings, waking to the sound of my mother humming to the kitchen radio while she prepared my breakfast. Was it okay to let someone else run the world again?

Whether I called it flying like a goose or following my child-like instincts, it meant knowing something greater than me was guiding the universe. A wise brother had posted on the bulletin board these words of St. Bernard of Clairvaux: "You will discover things in the woods that you never found in books. Stones and trees will teach you things you never heard from your schoolteachers." So when I spotted a patch of moss and wondered if it was really as soft as it looked, I bent to see for myself (it wasn't). When my feet, tired and dusty in my sandals, heard the sound of running water, I let them find it (and was reminded it was, only last week, ice). When offered cheese made by the monks, I ate it slowly, savoring every bit. Someone else made the moss, melted the ice, aged the cheese. My part was to touch, to splash, to taste. I didn't force gratitude, just chose to receive. To receive air I had not made into lungs I had not formed. Such receiving revealed grace in everything. Gratitude was inevitable.

The point here is not to force mountaintop experiences but to be present to the marvelous things at work in our ordinary daily experience, to be present to the miracle of God's creation and provision. Write a poem to describe one tiny blade of grass or the color of your mother's hair. Do a sketch of your own fingerprint or your favorite tree. Make recordings of all the local birds or walk your neighborhood to photograph tiny architectural details you usually overlook. Keep a journal by your bed to record your favorite moment of each day. As I write, my favorite green cardigan is on the back of my chair, my dog is snoring, and I can smell coffee brewing. What's happening right around you that is good or lovely? Think on these things.

Whimsy is wonderful. But this is so much more than whimsy. We create caricatures of children—they're either undisciplined terrors or playful sprites. I remembered my own childhood through a sentimental lens until a childlike whim led me to wander into a workshop where Katy Smith, an early childhood educator, shared the very significant leadership lessons she's learned from toddlers. She invited me to set aside my caricatures and to remember my actual experience of childhood. She reminded me that even in a troubled or traumatic childhood, as children we are alive and present and honest. She put it this way:

Toddlers own a room and assume that they are welcome. They're driven by intense curiosity and go for it without over-thinking. Toddlers insist that you shut out all other distractions to be with them, present and purposeful. They feed themselves—their bodies, minds, and souls—without apology. They take care of their needs. Toddlers understand how powerful words are and are not afraid to say the hard things or the joyful things. They will tell you when they are hurting and will look for support. They wear band-aids proudly to remind us all that they are

> "God is waiting for human human beings."
>
> Jürgen Moltmann, *The Source of Life:*
> *The Holy Spirit and the Theology of Life*

recovering from something that hurt them. Toddlers will let you know when they need to be carried. They ask for grace when they need to be understood and accepted. Toddlers embrace the need to melt down and do not see their emotions as a weakness but as an effective tool to communicate with the people who care for them. Toddlers comfort themselves when they are uncertain, scared, or lonely. They're not ashamed to need comfort to get through hard times. Toddlers trust in their ability to be at the top of the curly slide. They assume competence and self-correct when they have misjudged a situation.[2]

When children are tired or sick, they rest—without feeling like failures. When they need help, they ask for it. Children are receptive; their hearts and senses and instincts are always on. And they pay attention to what these parts of them reveal about themselves and the world around them—whether it is hurt feelings or a caterpillar, it is significant and requires investigation. And when children feel prompted by their instincts, they respond with courage. This is what it means to be human, and I want to be more like this (again). This is not a new skill. We've been this before.

Healing to Fragmented Selves

Suddenly the Bible said things I'd never noticed before. How had I never seen how whole its characters were? How had I missed how very human their experiences were? Not only did the people in the Bible seem comfortable with their complete thinking, feeling, sensing human experience but the Bible gloried in the many ways humans express God's whole self. Scripture uses language for soul, spirit, mind, stomach, heart, and breast without our Western need to create hard categories and hierarchies. While the Hebrew and Greek words translated in these ways certainly have their own meanings, their semantic domains overlap—they are at home with one another in ways that make modern, Western, English speakers uncomfortable. When Jesus says we should love God with all our heart and soul and mind and strength (Mark 12:30; Luke 10:27), he is not creating a taxonomy but describing a kind of engagement that involves our whole selves. Paul regularly disturbs our modern desire to distinguish between mind and heart with passages like "I pray that the eyes of your heart may be enlightened" (Eph. 1:18). If we bring our hearts, minds, bodies, and spirits to our reading of Scripture, we may come to a more complete understanding than ever before.

Scripture is comfortable with the complex, multifaceted beings we are. It tells stories of humans engaging with their whole selves and a God who engages with his whole self. It is only in recent history that we have become uncomfortable with these parts of Scripture, ourselves, and God. As Rollo May describes it,

> The chief characteristic of the last half of the nineteenth century was the breaking up of personality into fragments. These fragmentations . . . were symptoms of the emotional, psychological, and spiritual disintegration occurring in the culture and in the individual. . . . The Victorian man saw himself as segmented into reason, will, and emotions and found the picture good. . . . [The] citizen of the Victorian period so needed to persuade himself of his own rationality that he denied the fact that he had ever been a child or had a child's irrationality and lack of control; hence the radical split between the adult and

the child. . . . Kierkegaard and Nietzsche were keenly aware that the "sickness of soul" of Western man was a deeper and more extensive morbidity than could be explained by the specific individual or social problems. Something was radically wrong in man's relation to himself.[3]

John Wesley created a way to bring these parts of ourselves together as we discern how to follow God. The Wesleyan Quadrilateral names four elements to be considered in our discernment: Scripture, tradition, reason, and experience. While Scripture is the most authoritative, our interpretations of it are not, and we will understand it most faithfully when we bring in the history of our tradition, the voices of others, our God-given reason, and the ways we engage God in our daily experience. Few of us have a balanced approach to these parts of our experience.

As Scripture increasingly began to speak to my entire lived experience, I longed to figure out how to engage Scripture with less shame for those experiences that come as tears or dancing before they can ever be words. I wanted to know how to welcome the ways God begins with songs and dreams and groans. I began to see that my reverence for truth-as-printed-text had kept me from seeing how much Scripture itself tells stories of truth embodied. I began to ask, "What if those parts of myself that I find embarrassing, confusing, annoying, or distasteful are places where God longs to connect with me? What if these are places where God drops a tiny taste of his own longings to

FIELD GUIDE

How have you experienced this segmenting of the self? How have you seen or experienced this "sickness of the soul" as a result?

flavor our ways of knowing? What if on a daily basis I say no to these ways God wants to meet with me and love me?"

As messy as it was, figuring this out was no longer optional. If the presence of God is now expressed on earth in our bodies, and if the world will know the redemption of God through that Spirit's expression through our words and lives, I needed to know that Spirit within me. If that Spirit doesn't make hard distinctions between thinking, feeling, and sensing, I wanted to set aside those barren boxes to learn how to partner with this mysterious force at work in me. It was deeply unnerving to press "pause" on my own control and wait on something that may or may not reveal itself and accept that even when it does it still may not make sense. But I decided that discomfort was no reason to avoid the lesson.

Right about now I started to wonder if I was "going charismatic." I come from a tradition that absolutely positively is pretty sure that miracles are no more and trusts that God reveals himself only through the printed text of the Bible. That represents a kind of prideful certainty that isn't very Christian. Surprisingly, I find a similar but opposite certainty in some folks who talk about the Spirit all the time—it's tempting to be absolutely positively pretty sure exactly what God will do and what he's saying to everyone around us. Both extremes hold their own agendas and seek to retain control, claiming certainty when we should have a reverence for all that could be and all we don't know. What I began to see in people who really know the Spirit is a daily discernment, a watching and a waiting and a turning over whatever comes their way. It leads them to be humble and self-aware and comfortable with vagueness. It forces a daily conversation with God and Scripture and the community of believers. All of this sounds very slow and messy. And wonderful.

My upbringing and culture have taught me that from the moment I open my eyes each morning, the world is what I make of it. What this day will be is mine to create, what my work and relationships will be is mine to control. Even if I never say with my mouth "It's all up to me," my life had been saying "It's all up to me" in how I fretted over the things I feel responsible for, in how I was made uncomfortable by every detail of life I couldn't understand or control. And the amount of energy I devoted to blaming myself when I failed finally made these unspoken beliefs apparent. I began to wonder: "What might it be like every morning to open my eyes to a world already humming along and to wonder how to join in the humming?"

Rest from Deity

The challenge that God presented to the people of Israel was to wake in this way of wonder at least one day out of every seven. Even if our Sabbath keeping is not an entire day, we still need Sabbath. We still need time to figure out how to let God run the world, whether it's for one minute an hour, one hour a day, or one day a week. There's a reason God invited the people into Sabbath before he gave them the Law. And there's a reason God got seriously vexed when the Israelites ignored Sabbath keeping. Sabbath is not just a day off. Sabbath is about life and death. In fact, I've heard it said that in Sabbath God invites us to practice for our own death in two ways: to get used to being in God's presence for the pure sake of it (as we will be in the afterlife) and to learn to trust he can carry the world without us (as he'll continue to do after we have passed).[4] Whether or not we devote an entire day out of seven to this practice, in a culture that tempts us to be God we need this kind of sobering rehearsal more than ever. Even if they're stolen between the "significant" things in life, these moments to step aside and pay attention might release us from the need to be God and let us live as whole humans again. And although it has to begin by setting aside time, a swinging from working to resting, the more we practice it, the more the rest stays with us even when we're productive. We begin to do our work with an awareness that we're not making this world but joining God in the work of remaking it. The mental, physical, and emotional restoration we gain from resting is only part of the point. The habit helps us rest from our own striving toward deity.

To be so open to God, so aware of my place in the world, and so awake to my own self seemed wonderful but out of reach. Once I became convicted of how much I'd been striving in my own strength, I wanted to change. But how could I remake myself into this new self? Surely it would take years to accomplish this reconstruction work! That self-starter compulsion runs deep. The child in me posed a new possibility: "What if this is an invitation to even set aside the habit of making yourself?" I suddenly found that I had what I'd needed all along. There's a slumbering child in each of us who knows these ways to not be

FIELD GUIDE

While you may not have total control over your ability to rest, especially if your work places certain demands on you, what do you do with the time you can control? Even in your "rest" do you stay in a productivity rut? Or maybe you only value rest in its ability to make you more productive when you return to work.

Stuart Brown, director of the National Institute for Play, lists eight Play Personalities: The Joker, The Kinesthete, The Explorer, The Competitor, The Director, The Collector, The Artist/Creator, and The Storyteller.[5] Which of these describes your play as a child? Even children with unhappy childhoods had moments to themselves to direct their own lives. How did you spend that time? What would it look like for the adult version of you to reawaken your play personality?

God. As I let her rub the sleep from her eyes, she began to show me that being in God's presence for the sake of it and letting God carry the world would not feel so much like death after all. That if there were ways God wanted me to grow, he could allow those to unfold over my entire life. It wasn't my job to remake myself but to say yes to how he wanted to remake me.

It began in slow, sleepy ways; in still, small voices; in tiny, unspeakable urges that I'd belittled and ignored. The world that told me life is entirely what I make of it had no time for these foolish feelings and prompts. But this was a moment to embrace "small" things. It began with giving my ears the time to alight on every note in a bird song before I launched out of bed and into "big, important" things. It began with lingering to savor the smell of warm skin, with paying attention to a Bible word that snagged on my heart. A tabletop suggested its grain needed my touch. The sky needed me to pull out of traffic for two minutes to watch how it ended the day. A thousand worms marooned on a rainy driveway needed to be saved, slowly, with a stick and great care. They needed it so much and for so long that I didn't even notice the snickering of onlookers.

Loving as a Way to Know

This kind of openness and responsiveness transformed my entire way of engaging with the world. It taught me to value input before I could explain why it was valuable and opened my eyes to truth beyond the things I thought I understood. It was an expansive landscape but the same openness that made anything possible in all the best ways, made anything possible in all the worst ways. Would this new way of being cause me to lose friends and respect? My exhilaration at new possibilities was tainted by fear and loneliness. It was perfect timing for finding a new friend, the wise and gentle Christian epistemologist Esther Lightcap Meek. She has a name for what I was beginning to do. She calls it "Loving to Know," and it has given me permission to approach life as an adult who is as open as a child. She writes, "Reality is not such that we can exhaust it. Reality is continuously dynamic, ever-new gift. It harbors mystery and surprise, always. But we and it are meant to trust each other and thrive in that trust. This is the joy of communion. And while life and knowing is often thwarted and broken and difficult, we still have a choice how to view it as we set about knowing. Choosing dancing toward communion invites the real. It makes us better knowers even as it makes us better lovers."[6]

To love in order to know, we have to welcome two kinds of input: primary and subsidiary. Primary input is what is at the center of our attention while subsidiary input comes from awareness of who is around us, the things our bodies are sensing, what is going on in our surroundings. These are ways of learning that we knew and trusted as children. They're not in conflict with focal things, and we can add them without setting aside what our education and experience have taught us. I began to discover that I could engage as a whole being by bringing all these pieces together and being open to a God who speaks through Scripture, music, conversation, ideas, feelings, instincts, intellect, nature, and bodily experience. It began to awaken parts of me lying dormant. It began to reveal a God much more multidimensional than I ever knew.

This permission to engage with my whole self made me want to revisit Jesus's ways of talking about children. I'd often seen his comments about children as soft-focus, throwaway sentiments. It is easy to imagine that Jesus just chose to use the ragamuffins milling about to gather the crowd's attention since the kids' antics were already causing a distraction. It's tempting to take the passing nature of his comments about children as a sign of their insignificance. And yet his brief statements may take the rest of our lives to fathom.

Just before he mentions the children in Luke 18, Jesus has been telling the story of the Pharisee and the tax collector. While it's in the form of a parable, we can easily imagine the scene unfolding as Jesus speaks. Jesus describes two men going to the temple to pray, one a Pharisee—an insider, the apparent good guy—and the other a despised tax collector. And yet Jesus is unimpressed with the prayers of the Pharisee, who is so convinced of his own completeness that there's no need for God (except to thank God that he is not like the tax collector nearby). Meanwhile, the tax collector, unaware of the Pharisee's scorn, pours out his heart to God from a profound awareness of his reliance on the Lord's mercy. What is happening in the heart of the tax collector that is not happening in the heart of the Pharisee? What allows the tax collector to be so responsive?

What a surprising story in which the Pharisee with all his religious learning has become the object of reproach while the tax collector is the unlikely hero. Luke provides some insight, explaining that Jesus told this parable "for some who trusted in themselves." Perhaps those self-assured folks are still within hearing when Jesus then turns to the children clambering onto his lap and the lesson continues. When the disciples try to shoo away the children, Jesus says what could be one of his most significant yet least considered statements:

> Let the little children come to me, and do not hinder them, for the kingdom of God belongs to such as these. Truly I tell you, anyone who will not receive the kingdom of God like a little child will never enter it. (Luke 18:16–17)

We may sigh, "Aww, how nice. Jesus likes the little kiddies," and promptly move on to more important passages that can be built up into more serious theologies. Children are cute and all, but you really want us to be like that, Jesus? Don't you know, Jesus, that children are small and unruly, weak and uninformed?

We have important things to do because other people are counting on us. So we read this passage in passing. We miss his joyful, weighty invitation. What if it really is true that we cannot receive or enter God's kingdom unless we are like a child? If it were true, and we really wanted God, wouldn't we spend a little more energy exploring this strange but very clear statement? Like Nicodemus, wouldn't we ask with real urgency, "How can someone be a child when they're grown? Surely we can't turn back the clock!" What if a thorough, courageous investigation of this conundrum might take us another way to the place we are so desperately trying to find? I've devoted the rest of my life to the exploration of these questions.

The only thing Jesus really talked about was God's kingdom—the place where a reign of peace is possible. He invited humans, fettered by reigns of domination, discord, and scarcity, to imagine a possibility of power without abuse. It seems to me that if we really longed for such a place, we'd hang on every instruction Jesus gave for how to get there. He did give a clear instruction: be like a child. But that's just asking too much (or perhaps too little?). The invitation to become like children is so preposterous that we dismiss it without a thought. Being a child is never the way to important things. So we ignore Jesus's way and set about finding our own way into the kingdom, which amounts to taking the kingdom by force. Although we want a place without the abuse of power, we work to get there through abuse of our own small power. Our well-intentioned pursuit of God becomes a hunt. Our honest desire to partake of God becomes consumption. Our attempts to grasp him turn into domination. We're surprised when all our efforts fall flat—God just seems powerless and his kingdom feels like a farce—because *how* we do things cannot be separated from what we're trying to do.

What if the door to the kingdom is so small that all our efforts to puff ourselves up to be good enough to enter actually disqualify us instead? Perhaps the door is the eye of a needle for everyone. The question is whether we'll continue to persist in being camels. Immediately after Jesus invites his hearers to receive the kingdom like a child, a wealthy man asks how to enter the kingdom. Jesus offers this ridiculous image of a large beast squeezing through a tiny space, hard enough to thread with even just one camel's hair. Is Jesus asking us to submit to what will feel like cruel surgery? Is he saying that we can enter only by amputating essential parts of ourselves? Or is he releasing us from our habits of being something we were never meant to be? When we have been freed of our self-sufficiency, our habits of "fix, control, comprehend," we will find ourselves small enough to enter and empty enough to receive. When we have repented of both our deflated inactivity and our puffed-up overactivity we will remember how to engage as collaborators again. If we take the risk to do it the way Jesus says—by being like children—the pure discomfort of it will remake us into kingdom dwellers. The kingdom is already here. We may need to be transformed to enter it.

This is the posture that God has invited us into throughout the history of his engagement with humans. He longed for Israel to enter this relationship as his children. They preferred legalism, power, foreign gods—all more satisfying than entering into love as recipients. When they had stoned every prophet who called them back to God's heart, he entered the world to model how he longs for us to approach him. Jesus knows his need for the Father, acknowledges his reliance on the Father, seeks the Father's comfort and guidance, and gives the Father credit for the power. He was a true human, more human than we dare to be. And if we choose not to be ashamed of Jesus's childlikeness toward the Father, we too find the capacity to become small enough to be children of God.

This humility, this childlikeness, is both simple and impossible. Jesus says so himself. No amount of cleverness or resourcefulness or sheer force on a camel's part will squeeze it through the eye of a needle. For good reason the disciples respond with exasperation: "Then who can be saved?" (Luke 18:26). But Jesus defies their desire for an easy resolution by answering the question he wishes they'd asked, inviting them to consider who God is instead of who they are not: "What is impossible with man is possible with God" (18:27).

We would rather be given action steps than be asked to rely on God. Compared to the ridiculous effort of pulling ourselves up by our own bootstraps, childlikeness could feel like relief from anxious striving. But to those accustomed to their own efforts, more often it feels like a cruel conundrum. We ricochet between "It's all up to God" and "It's all up to me," neither of which actually requires much engagement with God. Our work is not to be strong and smart enough but to stop working so hard. And, at the same time, our work is not to delegate all responsibility to God. Total passivity or total self-reliance are not our only options. Our part is to release our tight grip on this life we think is ours, keeping our hands open to receive back whatever he decides is our part, every day. Will we allow him to make us small enough to enter the kingdom? And once in the kingdom, will we be willing to grow into the fullness of our calling as "a kingdom and priests to serve" him, to "reign on the earth" (Rev. 5:10)?

Jesus's Childlikeness

We know how to live as though "It's all up to God" or "It's all up to me." What is harder to imagine is this third way. Thankfully, we don't have to only imagine it since we have a model in Jesus's own childlikeness toward the Father. In his sermon "The Child in the Midst," George MacDonald explores why Jesus had such high regard for the way of children: "To receive a child in the name of Jesus is to receive Jesus; to receive Jesus is to receive God; therefore to receive the child is to receive God himself."[7] What a wonderful invitation: to learn childlike humility from a God who is not only willing to welcome children but also willing even to become a child.

If we watch closely how Jesus is like a child toward the Father, we may understand what Jesus is asking of us. In one of the few books that examine Jesus's call to childlikeness, Hans Urs von Balthasar takes time to describe the four traits of childlikeness that are evident in Jesus.[8] As we imagine this whole being Balthasar paints, we see how relationship between God and human beings is possible again.

First, *Jesus knows his place and receives it with peace*. His trust in the goodness of the Father leads Jesus to live in deference to him: "The Son can do nothing by himself; he can do only what he sees his Father doing, because whatever the Father does the Son also does. For the Father loves the Son and shows him all he does" (John 5:19–20). While this is a posture of humility, it is not one of humiliation. Jesus empties himself of all for the Father, trusting that the Father will also fill. It is nothing less than love freely given and freely received in pure openness.

Second, *Jesus's essential stance toward the Father is thanksgiving*. His awareness of his need for the Father makes him always grateful for the Father's provision, always reliant on him, and always ready to give to others. "Because he is needy he is also thankful in his deepest being. . . . To be a child means to owe one's existence to another, and even in our adult life we never quite reach the point where we no longer have to give thanks for being the person we are."[9] From Jesus's gratitude and sense of need grows his deep generosity.

Third, *Jesus not only approaches the Father in humility and gratitude, he knows the intimacy he shares with all children of God, his brothers and sisters*. He is able to guide and teach others while also being in submission to the Father, remembering what it means both to be obeyed and to obey. He sees himself as a child of the Father without losing sight of the broader family to which he belongs—I in thee and thee in me and us in them and them in us (John 17:21–22).

And finally, *Jesus is at peace with the limitations of time and so lives in the fullness of the moment.* He is fully alive, attentive to the work of the Father and the needs of his brothers and sisters. His submission to this kind of childlikeness allows him to be fully human: "The child has time to take time as it comes, one day at a time, calmly, without advance planning or greedy hoarding of time. Time to play, time to sleep. . . . Play is possible only within time so conceived, and also the unresisting welcome we give to sleep. And only with time of this quality can the Christian find God in all things, just as Christ found the Father in all things."[10]

Jesus seems to be at peace with being childlike. We don't always experience that peace. One thing I learned when I started talking about childlikeness is how often people want to clarify, "But mind you're not child*ish*." We are more attentive to Paul's mention of putting away childish things than we are to Jesus's instruction to become like children. (As we will see, the two can coexist.) As much as this invitation toward childlikeness drew me in, there was serious internal and external resistance. I didn't yet know the difference between childlikeness and childishness, but I knew Jesus knew it. He reveals to us the beauty of a life lived, knowing how we fit into the broader whole—in harmony with the Father and with one another. He feels no need to selfishly withdraw in childish ways or to force himself on others in adultish ways. He can hover in a space of needing and being needed, of serving and being served, knowing and living within his limitations. He does not even feverishly work at making himself more childlike. He is a human at peace. A true self.

In describing Jesus's own childlikeness, Balthasar gives us a clearer path to follow as we try to respond well to Jesus's call to childlikeness. As we see every story of Jesus through this lens, it's easier to imagine Jesus's kind of humility, gratitude, relational intimacy, and attentiveness. Balthasar's picture of Jesus makes me want to live like that. But sadly, I'm left where Christian study often leads me: working hard to make myself like Jesus. My Western performance habits are triggered by Balthasar's list of attributes, and I'm sent right back to where I started—engaging adultish ego to make myself more childlike. As helpful as books are, Jesus doesn't say "*think* about being like a child" but "*be* like a child." All our well-intentioned efforts keep us busy at the door to the kingdom. All our work to attain childlikeness does not help us to actually enter.

There are things we won't learn about Jesus's invitation until we embrace how we learned and lived as children. This hopeful new possibility is raised by The Child Theology Movement. This new conversation, growing from a Malaysian gathering of Christian practitioners and theologians, asks: "As Jesus did something highly significant with a child in Matthew 18, as children make up about half the world's population, as they are the most oppressed social group and as we all are or have been children, isn't it time that we brought this perspective to bear on our understanding of what is meant by 'the kingdom of God' and how we are to live in God's way?"[11] Those involved in this hopeful new movement ask us to reconsider our very way of thinking about theology. They propose that we might learn something about the kingdom not only by studying how to be more childlike from a posture of adulthood (which usually studies from a safe distance, pretending to be objective) but also by truly being like them. "The child is capable of breaking through our theologies and habits of mind. . . . Jesus places the child in the midst of an argument about greatness in the kingdom of God, expecting the child to make a crucial difference to the argument."[12]

If Jesus really meant that we need to be like children to enter the kingdom, then that deserves serious attention. And we give serious attention in the way adults do: we shoo the children from the room and set aside our bodily needs and emotional whims so we can engage without interruption (albeit with only a small part of ourselves). Egos and intellects are welcome. They help us dissect and debate. They make us feel objective and strong. But when Jesus's disciples started in that direction, he refused to be wrapped up in it. He disrupted their whole way of engaging not by presenting a perfectly worded treatise but by simply plopping a messy, curious little being right into the middle of their debate. Any treatise would have only perpetuated their existing worldview; instead, Jesus turns a soft eye toward a small person, opening a window to an entirely new world.

What might we learn by bringing childlikeness in its natural state to the center of the conversation? What might our own childlike questions, interests, and values bring to our understanding of God? Is it okay to welcome these parts of ourselves? Considering the possibility seems both ridiculous and too good to be true. Becoming like children is not regression. To be like children is to be human again: awake to the whole experience of dwelling in bodies and in the world and unsurprised that we are incomplete and attuned to our need for something beyond ourselves.

Thomas Merton is, for me, one of the greatest examples of a truly human Christian thinker—a man whose rigorous theological inquiry meant bringing all he was. One of his most important works ends with this observation:

> What is serious to men is often very trivial in the sight of God. What in God might appear to us as "play" is perhaps what He Himself takes most seriously. At any rate the Lord plays and diverts Himself in the garden of His creation, and if we could let go of our own obsession with what we think is the meaning of it all, we might be able to hear His call and follow Him in His mysterious, cosmic dance. . . . We are invited to forget

ourselves on purpose, cast our awful solemnity to the winds and join in the general dance.[13]

I wonder if Merton had learned these lessons in the same Abbey woods that had been teaching me. It wasn't hard to imagine he'd cast his solemnity to the same winds.

It's no coincidence that I was finding friends in monks. While these approaches seemed new and strange to me, the contemplative tradition has been exploring them for centuries. And the more I learn about these seemingly lofty practices of contemplation, the more I see that those who are really "good" at it are so because they have learned to stop trying so hard to be good at it. They are grounded, human, attentive, receptive— childlike. James Finley describes the ways he was trained in contemplation by Merton himself: "Here's a first indication of what it means to live a contemplative way of life: It is to have a faith that our own heart in its most childlike hour did not deceive us."[14] Merton models this way of life so well because he embodies many things that seem to be in conflict: an artist and scholar, a thinker and feeler, a writer and a romantic, a man of action who knew how to need God, a world-changer who had not forgotten how to wander in the woods. And so, as a responsible adult, learning to respond as a child, I need his words: "Contemplation is . . . life itself, fully awake, fully active, fully aware that it is alive. It is spiritual wonder. It is

FIELD GUIDE

What about this invitation makes you hesitate? What excites you? What is in conflict in you as you imagine what it might mean to engage with God and one another as whole beings?

spontaneous awe at the sacredness of life, of being. It is gratitude for life, for awareness and for being. . . . [Contemplation]
is a pure and a virginal knowledge, poor in concepts, poorer
still in reasoning, but able, by its very poverty, and purity, to
follow the Word wherever He may go."[15]

Merton proposes a new possibility that feels too good to be
true. When first venturing into this exploration of childlikeness, I'd imagined a Grown-Up God releasing me to go and
play: "You go explore the world while I run it without you
for a while." What I was surprised to find, after being given
leave by Sustainer God, was Delighter God, at play in his own
creation, inviting me to join. I had not expected that this whim-
sical "waste of time" might lead me into deeper communion
with no less than the Creator of all things. G. K. Chesterton
paints the picture of a God who is not too important to enjoy
his own work.

> Because children have abounding vitality, because they are in
> spirit fierce and free, therefore they want things repeated and
> unchanged. They always say, "Do it again"; and the grown-
> up person does it again until he is nearly dead. For grown-up
> people are not strong enough to exult in monotony. But perhaps
> God is strong enough to exult in monotony. It is possible that
> God says every morning, "Do it again" to the sun; and every
> evening, "Do it again" to the moon. It may not be automatic
> necessity that makes all daisies alike; it may be that God makes
> every daisy separately but has never got tired of making them.
> It may be that He has the eternal appetite of infancy; for we
> have sinned and grown old, and our Father is younger than
> we.[16]

We find ourselves with a choice to make: Do we do what
we've always done and get the same, sad outcomes? Or do we
rest from our efforts at "making reality" and truly engage the
Reality already surging in and around us? The challenge is not

to attain some new skill or knowledge but to abandon our habit of attaining and to remember old ways we knew as children, which our Christian forebears knew and are still practiced by Christian adults in other traditions and cultures. If our culture, our upbringing, our education, our socialization, and the media all shape us into makers and doers, strivers and achievers, this childlike posture will be strange. As Hans Urs von Balthasar puts it, "It may be that this Christian requirement to keep our divine childlikeness alive in all areas of our existence becomes more difficult the more technical man seeks to shape and govern everything on his own."[17] More difficult, yes, but not impossible when Reality within us constantly urges us to engage Reality all around us.

I cannot express how strange and terrifying this was. But I'd caught a glimpse of something that seemed worth the risk. To name what I was embracing, I wrote a kind of covenant. I offer it here as a summary but also as an invitation for you to embrace it with me (or write your own).

> I choose to pay attention to the small things that are calling for my attention, even when I'm trying to do big things.
>
> I choose to trust that these small things can find me in moments when I actually have a minute to give (even if I don't feel like I do), and I choose to trust that my life will not fall to pieces if I stop for a moment to pay attention.
>
> I choose to listen to my senses, my emotions, my instincts, to engage the world with my whole self.
>
> I will not force these moments to arrive on my time or to mean what I want them to mean. I choose to set aside my striving for "big" things and choose to attend to the small, kingdom things in small, kingdom ways.

I trust that real things are hidden in surprising places, even
    if others around me don't see it.

I trust that Reality is at work all around and within me,
    waiting for me to join it.

I choose to forget myself. On purpose.

And join in the general dance.

▶ Creed

I believe in the life of the word,
the diplomacy of food. I believe in salt-thick,
ancient seas and the absoluteness of blue.
A poem is an ark, a suitcase in which to pack
the universe—I believe in the universality
of art, of human thirst
for a place. I believe in Adam's work
of naming breath and weather—all manner
of wind and stillness, humidity
and heat. I believe in the audacity
of light, the patience of cedars,
the innocence of weeds. I believe
in apologies, soliloquies, speaking
in tongues; the underwater
operas of whales, the secret
prayer rituals of bees. As for miracles—
the perfection of cells, the integrity
of wings—I believe. Bones
know the dust from which they come;
all music spins through space on just
a breath. I believe in that grand economy
of love that counts the tiny death
of every fern and white-tailed fox.

I believe in the healing ministry
of phlox, the holy brokenness of saints,
the fortuity of faults—of making
and then redeeming mistakes. Who dares
brush off the auguries of a storm, disdain
the lilting eulogies of the moon? To dance
is nothing less than an act of faith
in what the prophets sang. I believe
in the genius of children and the goodness
of sleep, the eternal impulse to create. For love
of God and the human race, I believe
in the elegance of insects, the imminence
of winter, the free enterprise of grace.

Abigail Carroll, *Habitation of Wonder*
(Eugene, OR: Cascade, 2018), 115–16.
Used by permission of Wipf & Stock
(www.wipfandstock.com).

CHAPTER 2

What Gets in the Way of Rest

In case I've given you the impression this experience was all mountaintops and monks, it's probably important to share how much all of this listening to incomprehensible prompts made me squirm. There were many good reasons I hadn't listened to those urges for so long. As these childlike longings raised legitimate concerns of intellect, theology, power, and even existence, I had to face how many selves are in conflict within me.

Intellectual Concerns: What Counts as Reliable Information?

At this point I still imagined that I could dabble in some childlikeness while retaining comfort and control. But this dabbling in childlikeness not only provided new experiences for me to consume, it also turned me inside out. It awakened a part of me that had slipped into a coma—an honest, courageous, truth-seeking part that wanted to lead me through experiences that would break and remake me. And there were parts of me that wanted none of it.

As my "fly like that" commitment had me listening more and more to my childlike voice, there was another voice that felt her power slipping. It was a voice I'd trusted for years, an adultish version of me; let's call her Amanda—the name I use on my tax return. (I'm sorry if your name is Amanda. That may be the name of your true self. It wasn't mine.) She has little time or trust for anything rising up from gurgling places, things as subjective as urges or prompts. She trusts things that can be articulated clearly in words. She works tirelessly to sort through the messes of emotion until they can be spoken in a nice English sentence. When emotion can behave itself, then she'll let it come to the table. But the grunts of primitive instinct are never welcome. They must have nice manners and speak in complete sentences before they're invited. Tidy thinking is always welcome, and when emotion can settle itself down enough to join polite company, it is welcome as well. But what Amanda hasn't noticed is that this conversation is incomplete because it speaks only in sentences. I've had Dallas Willard's words quoted to me as a warning: "Feelings are, with a few exceptions, good servants. But they are disastrous masters."[1] But rarely has the quote included any reference to Willard's other warnings about overconfidence in our intellect or his invitations for us to engage as whole beings. Perhaps thoughts, instincts, and emotions are all good servants, and we need to learn how to listen to them all. The ancient Enneagram, a system of personality typing, gives voice to three equal parts of ourselves: head, heart, and gut. (Amanda cringes at the word "gut.") Gut gurgles and grunts. There's a way to welcome our whole selves, even the parts of ourselves that are unruly and embarrassing.

I've always been Amanda. My birth certificate says so. But there was a time before Amanda ran the show when I was comfortable with all parts of myself, trusted them and let them all speak into how to live this life. There was a time when Mandy knew that her body and her spirit and her mind and her instincts were in harmony, even if they didn't seem so at first. There was a time when Mandy knew God had given these to her to learn about life and about himself. I wanted to find Mandy again, to return to that kind of wholeness. I wanted to relearn those patient, listening skills my truer self knew, to learn how to respond to these instincts God had awakened in me. But I had no idea how to do that while still keeping up with my adult responsibilities. How could I live as an adult who is responsive to these risky childlike prompts? I journaled:

> During a difficult conversation today I felt a permission not to pursue an issue. I followed the instinct even though I can't explain it. Usually I would have the instinct but not act on it until I totally understood, but I'm learning that you often don't understand the wisdom behind instincts until you follow them. It leaves me wondering: How do I lead others and engage in relationships when I can't always explain my instincts? What if I decide to do something that people in my life don't get and I can't explain it to them? For most people I know "I felt prompted to" is not a good enough reason. Why should I expect others to take that as a good reason? It's not good enough for me either.

In Christian faith "I felt prompted to" is supposed to be a good reason, if not to do something, at least to *consider* doing

---

FIELD GUIDE

How do you usually respond to instinctive prompts? Do you know how to discern if they're from God or not? Even if they are from God, what makes you hesitate to listen to them or obey them?

something. While this language has been abused in so many ways, our movement is built on stories of how over many centuries God has prompted humans. While some have misused prompts as an excuse to ignore wisdom and Scripture, there may be new things we learn by bringing instincts, emotions, Scripture, and intellect together into our discernment.[2] In wrestling with this possibility it was helpful to read the words of social work researcher Brené Brown:

> What silences our intuitive voice is our need for certainty. Most of us are not very good at not knowing. We like sure things and guarantees so much that we don't pay attention to the outcomes of our brain's matching process. For example, rather than respecting a strong internal instinct, we become fearful and look for assurances from others. "What do you think?" "Should I do it?" "Do you think it's a good idea, or do you think I'll regret it?" "What would you do?" A typical response to these survey questions is, "I'm not sure what you should do. What does your gut say?" And there it is. *What does your gut say?* We shake our head and say, "I'm not sure" when the real answer is, "I have no idea what my gut says; we haven't spoken in years." When we start polling people, it's often because we don't trust our own knowing.[3]

What if we'll never discover a childlike connection with God until we remember the skill of carefully attending to prompts that don't come as words in our brains but as instincts in our guts? When presented with this possibility, I found myself torn between a hunger for certainty and a longing to explore where these prompts were leading. I wanted to trust that just as God is One, unable to contradict himself, so we have inherent integrity—minds can be one with guts. I felt invited to journey with God into the land beyond my comfort but wanted to know where he would lead before I followed. It terrified me, but I could not say no.

Theological Concerns: Is This Heresy?

The kind of theology that has grown out of the Western tradition is naturally going to trust its own methods: to reason is to find Truth, to find Truth is to reason. Any lack of understanding is a sign that more reading, talking, reasoning, or writing is in order. We are so steeped in this tradition that we rarely wonder if there are broader, better approaches to the study of God. And we rarely wonder if our way of studying God is truly scriptural. What if the very method of our study limits the outcomes? What if we're caught in a closed system and Jesus wants to release us from it?

Our study of God has too often been a kind of colonization, bringing not only our preconceived notions but also our deeply ingrained research practices to his mysteries. The history of the European colonization of Australia is a story of one failed expedition after another, of explorers venturing into the harsh expanses of the outback, weighed down by the assumption that study always requires French-polished writing desks and fully stocked stationery cabinets. Their small-minded approach to learning left a trail of absurd furniture strewn across the desert, a long line of jetsam full stopped with the explorer's own remains. Such efforts at clarity only created more mess. In the same way, our old habits, small imaginations, and large egos have limited our ways of understanding God. We've set off on our learning ventures in the same old ways, with the same old tools, retaining control of the outcomes. And like those ill-fated efforts at exploration, something dies in the process. As Christian columnist Andrée Seu Peterson puts it, "When 'first love' dies, Christianity does not go away; it becomes Western theology. To be specific, it morphs into a delight in systems and controversies and subtle semantic distinctions. Not able to bear the truth of an emptiness at the core, we surround the empty core with little projects and academic hobbies. No one will be

49

saved by it, of course."[4] In our effort to understand this thing that is supposed to save us, we've restrained its power. How can we ever be saved by something we've domesticated? There must be a way that allows salvation to actually have saving power.

With his language of empire, Walter Brueggemann helps me imagine a way to describe how, even as Christians, we're trapped in the power habits of the world. "[Our] technical way of thinking reduces mystery to a problem, transforms assurance into certitude, revises quality into quantity, and so takes the categories of biblical faith and represents them in manageable shapes."[5] Just as the people of Israel were dazzled by the worldly empires of their times—Egypt, Assyria, Babylon, Rome—we also get dazzled by the worldly empires of our day, although ours are harder to name. Anywhere there's commercial, industrial, military, economic, political, cultural, technological, or intellectual power we can be tempted by empire ways. As Western Christians, accustomed to these kinds of empire powers, it can be very difficult to discern how we bring them into our faith. Joerg Rieger's insight is helpful in revealing how this occurs:

> Empire . . . has to do with massive concentrations of power that permeate all aspects of life and that cannot be controlled by any one actor alone. . . . Empire seeks to extend its control as far as possible; not only geographically, politically, and economically . . . but also intellectually, emotionally, psychologically, spiritually, culturally, and religiously. . . . The problem with empire has to do with forms of top-down control. . . . [In] a situation of empire Christ becomes part of the system to such a degree that little or no room exists for the pursuit of alternative realities of Christ. Empire displays strong tendencies to domesticate Christ and anything else that poses a challenge to its powers.[6]

We can't overthrow empire. And we can't entirely disengage from it. But without even realizing it, we have brought its industrial-scale values into the yeast in the dough–scale kingdom of God. Ironically, even in our efforts to study the kingdom, we often have empire habits. We do kingdom things in empire ways. To enter the kingdom we'll need to remember how to do kingdom things in kingdom ways again. This will mean embracing story, substance, mystery, and a different kind of authority.

Engaging in this way will undoubtedly require rational thought and language, but it will not be satisfied with touching just a part of us. It will also draw in heart, body, and instinct. There will be no time for false dichotomies here that carve us up into tidy segments—no luxury to bring only a part of ourselves, no patience for being asked to choose thinking *or* feeling. No, that's the violent work of empire. In kingdom, we are invited as whole beings, and so we will need to remember curious and courageous ways from childhood and pair them with all our adult skills. What might our sense of smell teach us about the kingdom? What might our tears bring to our reading of Scripture? How might our dancing inform our doctrine? A child would know.

I see a longing for such an approach in the work of the Lived Theology movement: "In the end, how sincere we truly are, how desperate and committed we are, will be demonstrated by how hard we are on our discipline, how willing we are to break with academic fashion when fashion mutes the polyphonies of life, how willing we are to be honest and accept difficulty. . . . Lived theology emerges from the movements, transactions, and exchanges of the Spirit of God in human experience."[7] It is exhilarating to imagine that there may be ways to rigorously engage Scripture as whole beings, serious ways to study God that don't thwart his Spirit. I find it deeply satisfying that within the pages of the book *Lived Theology* (a title published by no less than Oxford University Press) there is an essay called "Theology without Footnotes" that charges us with the following:

> Dare to be subjective . . . as long as you're honest.
> Dare to use plain English—including the first-person perspective.
> Dare to tell stories. . . .
> Dare to delight in theology written—and lived.[8]

It's freeing at last to be given permission to do theology in a way that lives—to live theology. And as we do—whether we're in seminary or Sunday school—we shouldn't be surprised if it's risky and uncomfortable. Everything in our education has told us to avoid subjectivity, that our own intuitions are not good guides, that if we follow our senses and emotions we will become self-absorbed. And as if the inner critic is not enough, friends, even fellow Christians, may snicker at the foolishness of the very things that welcome the kingdom. We may be tempted to set aside these new ways for something that feeds the ego, soothes our need for certainty. Sensible self-talk may tell us this is a waste of time, that we're going to risk experiencing something only to come up empty-handed, feeling farther from God than we already felt.

Why do we allow ourselves to be so naively taken in by those skeptical voices and, at the same time, so staunchly critique the instincts that draw us toward joy? Is there a time to be critical of our critical thinking? It parades around with such airs of sophistication, puffed up by efforts at distance and objectivity, when under it all our small, human hearts just want to avoid being revealed, looking foolish, feeling disappointed. These hesitations at the door of new life may show us exactly how sad and small our way of living has been. Our serious, sensible empire habits have real ways of deriding the risky, vivid lives

God wishes for us. This is what it means to welcome the kingdom like a child—to risk loving something!

Is it too much to expect theologians to do their work in these risky ways? I get it: for theology departments to coexist in secular institutions they've had to toe some lines. At the same time, is it too much to ask those who have invested the most time in the study of God (and who shape our conversations about God) to be the ones who are most like him? I want the powers that shape Christian thinking to be held accountable to this standard of rigor. I want individual thinkers, teachers, and Bible readers to be released to embrace this way of studying and living, just as I want to choose this way of study and life myself.

> We will always need theologians who, under the invigorating power of the Holy Spirit, rigorously study the Scriptures and traditions of the church not just so we will "know" the truth but so we may live more truly and embody integrated minds, which will inevitably lead to mercy and justice. Good theology is not primarily about being right. It is about being good. The more that memory, emotion, attachment, and narrative are kept in view, the more theology will lead to the emergence of the mind of Christ and the strengthening of his body.[9]

If theological ideas are supposed to elucidate how God's character intersects with human experience, can intuitions and bodies and emotions be places where theological ideas can be tested and learned? We know that theology can reason and articulate. Can it also feel and breathe? We fear this might diminish theology. But what if it expands theology? What if it teaches us about a whole God who wants to engage us as whole beings, in every part of our existence? What if it shows the Bible to be a living, active Word again and the Spirit to be comfortable in human skin again? Not only do we need this kind of theology, we need to *be* these kinds of theologians.

Thankfully, these kinds of theologians can be found in the Bible. I'm fascinated by one particular moment in the disciples' discovery of Jesus on the road to Emmaus. They have spent the day together discussing events and Scripture, exploring truth—a thoroughly "theological" day. And when they finally discover the Truth that has been walking with them all along they verify it in a way that seems strange: "Were not our hearts burning within us while he talked with us on the road and opened the Scriptures to us?" (Luke 24:32). Their bodily, intuitive, emotional experience of Truth does not undermine their acceptance of it but only adds to its veracity. It really is possible that Truth can be embodied.[10]

It is time to end the old empire dichotomies of rational versus experiential faith and subjectivity versus objectivity. These dichotomies ask us to choose one part of ourselves over another part, which is a kind of violence against the integrated beings God has made us to be and so a kind of violence against him. We are invited to leave behind partial engagement with God to embrace whole-person engagement. It's no less than the way Jesus lived: "Christ—despite all efforts to domesticate him—remains a stumbling block. He never quite fits in, to the surprise of his contemporaries, . . . to the surprise of . . . status quo institutions, and to the surprise of the ecclesial establishment."[11]

In serious theological contexts, the ghost of rationalism leans over our shoulders, shaming our small, human ways. It labels poetic, whole-person, childlike approaches as New Age mumbo jumbo, self-help psychobabble, navel-gazing emotional subjectivity. This system we've been shaped by has demeaning labels for everything (and everyone) outside of it, keeping us bound up in its limited ways. To step outside of this system is to risk being dismissed as weak, foolish, overly emotional, inconsequential. When I talk like this to educated Christian adults I'm often told, "Stop talking about yourself. I came to hear about God," as if we can ever know him without watching how he makes himself known to us (and *in* us). We've come so far in our study of Scripture that we've actually left behind that same Scripture that contains passages like Ephesians 3:16–19:

> I pray that out of his glorious riches he may strengthen you with power through his Spirit in your inner being, so that Christ may dwell in your hearts through faith. And I pray that you, being rooted and established in love, may have power, together with all the Lord's holy people, to grasp how wide and long and high and deep is the love of Christ, and to know this love that surpasses knowledge—that you may be filled to the measure of all the fullness of God.

This thing we're so desperately working to understand is beyond our grasp, so we grasp at it with the kind of power that crushes things. But according to passages like this, our ability to know comes as a gift, and the power we're promised is power to receive. And all this power and knowing will take place in parts of ourselves we may not value—inner selves and hearts. It will take all that we are to know all that he is. Perhaps our dismissal of childlikeness is a symptom of our derision of the mysteries of our own human experience. We're so repulsed by the subjective, messy, insubstantial ways of our own humanness that we can no longer be present in the place where God comes to meet us—in our very human hearts and bodies. Ultimately, a disembodied approach to theology is poor Christology. God's greatest expression of truth was a human person.

As we recover from our limited Western trust in propositional statements as the highest form of truth, it may comfort us to know that there are many serious thinkers who long for this wholeness. Richard Rohr affirms the need for both inner and outer authority:

> Only when inner and outer authority come together do we have true spiritual wisdom. Christianity in most of its history has

largely relied upon outer authority. But we must now be honest about . . . inner experience, which of course was at work all the time but was not given credence. In fact, we were told not to trust it! If you were Catholic, you were told to trust the Tradition as interpreted by the authorities; if you were Protestant you were told to trust the Bible, also as interpreted by your denominational authorities.[12]

Power Concerns: Who Gets to Decide Truth?

If Jesus himself describes a childlike reorientation that will prepare us to know the Creator, and if educated, highly regarded Christian thinkers like Rohr have space for this possibility, what's holding us back? I'd like to propose it has something to do with power. Jesus doesn't mention children in response to people who are too busy to enjoy creation. He mentions children in response to arguments over power and hierarchies.

In Matthew 18 the disciples' petty squabbling over who will be greatest in the kingdom finds a perfect counterpoint in the form of a small child. I hope it shut them up. I assume it seemed ridiculous to grown men. This little urchin is the answer? To be great we have to be like this? In his usual way, Jesus has questioned the question, posing a challenge not only to their thinking but to their whole way of being, their whole value system, their whole reason for asking questions in the first place. What will it take for us to humble ourselves like a child? Do we even know what humility is?

Once more we're stuck in caricatures. We hear "humble" and imagine Jesus calls us to a kind of sycophantic self-loathing. "Humble" brings to mind a history of self-flagellation[13] and words of derision flying from the mouths of preachers. We are worms, loathsome spiders, held over the pit of hell. As monk Michael Casey puts it, "The idea of 'humility' evokes the images of a moral tyranny which imparts only fear, guilt, and an abiding sense of failure. It has nothing of encouragement or warmth to offer, only a carping insistence on human sinfulness."[14] But we are still stuck outside of the kingdom's way of seeing smallness. Ironically, there's a surprising kind of ego in these warped understandings of humility because we're still at the center. When we discover we're not the best we're suddenly the very worst—now the best at being unworthy. Within a child's way of seeing, we're ordinary even in our ordinariness. Humility is simply acknowledging the truth—that we are small in power and understanding and that's okay. We did not generate our own selves and cannot, on our own, sustain ourselves, but we are invited to be in relationship with the One who did and does. We are invited to receive all sustenance, insight, and goodness as gifts from a source outside ourselves because we are too small to be self-sufficient. Not small and measly, or small and meaningless, or small and pitiful, but rather small and welcome, small and unafraid, small and free.

In the late twentieth century, postmodern thought entered into biblical studies, interrogating our methods. It began to ask who gets to say what the Bible means and if there is truly a way to be objective in our reading of Scripture. This questioning undermined hundreds of years of pretending we can hold our beliefs at arm's length, that we can separate ourselves from our bodies, our stories, and our experiences in order to arrive at an entirely rational reading of Scripture. "What we realize now is that such objectivity and neutrality is illusionary. . . . In order to continue the traditions of critical historical work in our own times, we need to include our own perspectives and biases into our research."[15] This postmodern approach brought autobiographical literary criticism into theological studies, asking theological thinkers to be self-aware, telling alongside their readings of the Bible the very subjective stories that shape their understanding of the text.[16] While some saw this as a threat to orthodoxy, it may help to remember that while this all seems very radical and new to modern minds it is not so different from the ancient Jewish art of midrash, which is "a way of inhabiting the text in order to deepen your understanding of it. . . . Conventional reverence means standing at a distance from the text so that the light is refracted through it, as through a stained-glass window. With midrash, you need to get much closer than that. You need to swallow the text whole, digest it, assimilate it, excrete it, walk around with it resonating inside you for hours and days, let it become your constant meditation and your unceasing prayer."[17] Unlike the reverence that venerates from afar, this kind of reverence is living sacrifice.

This approach, whether we come to it through ancient midrash or postmodern thought, seems to question our idea that there is one overarching narrative, an assumption that has been foundational to Christian faith. Christians who accept the authority of Scripture would accept that there *is* an overarching narrative, one story that is true for every human who has ever lived, and that this story is told in the Bible. What we acknowledge less often is that each limited human—even a human with deep knowledge and academic pedigree—has a limited perspective on that story. Or to put it positively: the experience of any one person, living in a particular time and place and body, forms a distinctive lens through which they view Scripture. This diversity in our readings of Scripture does not have to mean conflict but instead can offer a multifaceted reading of Scripture, shaping a multifaceted image of God.

"People crave objectivity because to be subjective is to be embodied, to be a body, vulnerable, violable."

Ursula LeGuin, *Dancing at the Edge of the World*

There are certainly readings that are not true to the text or to our Christian story, but there is space for more perspective than we usually welcome. This requires us to humbly read Scripture together, welcoming the experiences of others across times and places. Even the process of discerning how we listen together and what defines a true interpretation can shape us. Our subjectivity has been feared (and there are ways we can abuse it in our reading of Scripture), but if we submit to one another and the Spirit, we can find something of God in Scripture and in one another that we have never seen before.

One of the places I've found the most faithful attention to these issues is in the conversations shaped by Missio Alliance.[18] I was honored to be part of a symposium they hosted, discerning the challenges and opportunities for the church in this moment of history. Fifty male and female theologians and practitioners, representing a beautiful diversity of denominations, ages, and ethnicities, spent the day shaping a statement that included these prophetic words:

> We affirm that theology is living, communal, conversational, contextual, creative, and unfolding.
>
> We confess that we have excluded other voices, that we confuse knowledge with experience, that we use theology as power over and to judge.
>
> The Holy Spirit is convicting us to find new pathways to do theology, to build bridges between Word and World, and to do so by depending on the Holy Spirit for wisdom rather than our own constructions.
>
> The way forward will be found as we find new ways to do theology that are historic, living, communal, conversational, contextual, creative, and unfolding, trusting that uncommon collaboration will help us imagine the theology we have yet to do.[19]

This hopeful way forward will mean welcoming ways of understanding Scripture and of knowing God that will at first be strange and uncomfortable. We'll need to redefine wisdom and foolishness. We'll need to rethink who gets the first and last word. And beyond inviting other voices because it's trendy or fair, we'll discover that we need what has always been available in the voices we have excluded. It is humbling in the best possible way to discover how much we need one another to understand God. Here's where we begin to understand how, in addition to children, Jesus taught that the outcast understood the kingdom. Jesus knew that in every way any human has had to exist outside of power, they have had the opportunity to embrace the limitations inherent in human existence. "[Those] who do not meet the demands of the status quo and are repressed by it . . . have a wider set of options that transcend the system. In being pushed to the margins of the system the repressed not only gain an alternative perspective . . . but they also gain surplus energies and enjoyment that escape the powers that be."[20]

Power dynamics still require a choice, and being on the margins does not automatically guarantee a healthy approach to power.[21] Inasmuch as any human has retained the childlike skill of submitting to human limitations—whether as a disabled white man or a rich Asian woman—they have something to teach us about the kingdom of God. We all, through the limitations of our bodies and minds and hearts, have to eventually confront our own humanness in some way or other.[22] Some humans just have more (or earlier) opportunities than others to befriend those limitations.[23] Will we invite their childlike wisdom into our conversations about God and Scripture? Can we be unsurprised if not only their outcomes but their very methodology seems strange, perhaps even foolish, to us—particularly if they come with tears or dancing? When we're convicted of our empire habits, we don't need to despair. There are kingdom experts all around us.

This kind of humility, this partnering with God in the world and in others, will require us to resign our tireless trust in ourselves. This resignation is not optional. It's how we receive relationship with God, how we enter his kingdom. Learning to receive the warmth of a sun I had not formed on a shoulder I had not shaped was practice for receiving the kingdom. Stopping to receive the juice of a cherry I had not made with taste buds I had not invented was practice for receiving the kingdom. Letting a word from a psalm sink into my soul, allowing my heart to say "amen" to an ancient prayer, all this was practice to keep my eyes and ears and heart open for things beyond me that were always at hand. These moments offer opportunities for humans to practice how to be receptive to their God. Sometimes it leads to moments of wonder, sometimes it troubles us with things that aren't right in ourselves and in the world. When we rest, it always leads to Truth. When the kingdom breaks in, it always leads to reality. How can we rediscover that childlike capacity for the Real?

Existential Concerns: Will This Undo Me?

As my adultish Amanda false self felt her influence waning, she made herself heard in more and more desperate ways. Like when, on a seemingly harmless walk, I felt a strange closeness to a particular tree. I was feeling a little lonely and something about the tree looked friendly. A small place in my heart asked my legs to saunter over to the tree, invited my arm to wrap around the tree's trunk, my cheek to press against the bark for a while. Amanda had a few things to say: "Really? You want to hug a tree? Isn't that a bit of a cliché? We are more sophisticated than that. And what will it accomplish? We have important things to do. And what will people think? Odd people hug trees. Childish, small, insignificant, irrational outsiders hug trees. Nobody takes tree huggers seriously. You'll lose all that work you've done to perfectly curate your self-image and gain respect. But sure, you go hug a tree if that's what you really want."

And then, when my legs kept moving toward the friendly tree, that inner voice chimed in with a final attempt: "I'm just trying to protect you from disappointment. What if it turns out to be lame? You'll be left feeling deflated and foolish, hugging a dumb tree. And if the experience was supposed to teach you something about God and God doesn't show up in spectacular ways, you'll feel even more alone. Is that what you want? Don't come crying to me if it wasn't all you thought it would be!"

The only thing for it was to go ahead and hug that tree.

With voices like that in my head, I needed some serious allies in this new devotion to childlikeness. Once more, Walter Brueggemann's words were reassuring: "Hope . . . is an absurdity too embarrassing to speak about, for it flies in the face of all those claims we have been told are facts. Hope is the refusal to accept the reading of reality which is the majority opinion; and one does that only at great . . . existential risk."[24] Yes! What had begun with a seemingly harmless commitment to childlikeness was leading me toward what truly felt like existential risk. Amanda likes predictability, efficiency, having a good reputation, things she can manage and measure. On the other hand,

FIELD GUIDE

What's the difference between helpful, healthy, and responsible organizational skills and unhealthy efforts at control for the sake of control? What about the difference between healthy regard for the opinions of others and unhealthy people-pleasing? Think of examples of each from your own life. How do your efforts to control outcomes and appearances keep you from saying yes to God?

childlikeness, instincts, and geese all cause serious upheaval to her efforts at control. Heeding Amanda's cautious warnings had led to acceptance and comfort, so it made sense that turning down her voice felt risky. In some ways I'd prefer physical risk to the existential kind. Physical risk doesn't threaten to undo your very self.

We have foundational survival skills that go way beyond physical safety. These inner voices work to keep us socially safe, well respected, welcomed, emotionally stable, feeling sure in our identity as individuals and as part of society. Survival is so much more than staying alive physically. And we have each woven a delicate web from social mores, parental advice, and educational experiences that we use to position ourselves in what seems socially and emotionally safe (even if only in our own minds). This is the normal process of socialization for self-aware, relational creatures, but not all of it is healthy.

Now that I had a chance to critically look at the ways one part of me talked to another part of me, I discovered Amanda was running the show even though I would never consciously affirm her values. Now that I could name her beliefs, I certainly wouldn't say they were good theology. On a conscious level I tell myself, "My identity and safety are found in God." Yet I was living out an entirely different set of beliefs—that my security is very tenuous, my identity changes with every failure, and it's all up to me to protect myself on every level. On a conscious level I tell myself, "God is the creator and sustainer of all things." And yet I was busily trying to run the world. Soon I started to wonder where all this stopped being unhealthy self-talk and started being something more disturbing. I started to wonder if Amanda's fears made her a puppet to dark forces.

I've been disappointed. We all have. I've had moments that have brought me tumbling to the ground, embarrassed that I had set my expectations so high—that I'd splashed around joyfully in the paints only to end up with art that just looked dumb. So it's easier just to set lower, more reasonable expectations next time and stop making scriptural claims about God's power or goodness or providence. I never consciously made this decision to guard myself—self-preservation is a pretty effective compulsion. But it had made for faulty theology and very small prayers. Out of an unspoken choice to always protect myself from embarrassment or disappointment, I'd set low expectations for God. I'd begun living against my own theological claims that he is mysterious and all-powerful.

It's a natural self-preservation tactic to avoid all that risk by numbing ourselves to vulnerability. Better to have a predictable, mediocre existence and avoid failure and foolishness than leap in with both feet. Childlikeness is risky—the possibility of hope also exposes us to the possibility of disappointment. We might risk caring about things bigger than ourselves. Amanda wanted to placate me. Amanda thought she was being helpful by steering me away from experiences that might expose my human weakness, and I was more than happy to play along if it meant I got to save face. But I was beginning to learn that "numbing vulnerability is especially debilitating because it doesn't just deaden the pain of our difficult experiences; numbing vulnerability also dulls our experiences of love, joy, belonging, creativity, and empathy. We can't selectively numb emotion. Numb the dark and you numb the light."[25]

Healing the Hesitations

All these concerns of intellect, theology, power, and existence had me at a standstill. Until I danced. One of the recurring instincts in my childlike moments on sabbatical had been a prompt to dance. Which, like most prompts, made no sense. But, out of obedience, I began reading about how dance is used in Scripture. I was really getting the hang of this thinking-about-dancing thing. Then a moment came at a wedding reception, when everyone else at my table headed for the dance floor. As I sat there alone, I sensed God saying, "It's not just a metaphor, you know." And so, although I hadn't danced for decades and wasn't sure if it's what wedding officiants do, and although I was self-conscious about my 1980's "moves," I danced. This act of obedience was awkward but fun, and that seemed the point—and the end—of that prompt. Until it came back to me well after my sabbatical was done.

A few Sundays after returning to work, the Sunday worship service included a reading of James 5:14: "Is anyone among you sick? Let them call the elders of the church to pray over them and anoint them with oil in the name of the Lord." As I heard these words, my mind turned to Laura, a deeply unwell woman in our congregation. I felt that same childlike urge that I'd promised to heed when it led me to drag a stick along a fence. Now it was prompting in new ways, to draw me out of many places of stuck-ness. Now I felt led to take this passage seriously on Laura's behalf and just as quickly I thought, "Yeah, nah. We don't do that kind of healing prayer thing around here. That's for the Pentecostal types. And anyway, what if we look dumb? What if God doesn't heal and we make him look bad? What if we get our hopes up and we're disappointed?" I set it aside. But the next day I made the mistake of mentioning this impulse to another church member, and when he said, "That reading also made me think we should pray for Laura!" we knew we had to do it. So I put out the word that we'd be gathering to pray for our friend, and as word spread other folks said, "Actually, I've been wanting to ask for healing prayer too." So instead of a quiet time of prayer for one woman that could easily remain small and low-key (i.e., easily let go of if it "failed"), now it had become a healing prayer service, not only the first I'd ever led but the first I'd ever attended.

As the hour of this healing prayer service approached, I felt God daring me again to dance. As if leading the service wasn't enough risk, now my obedience had to involve the added weirdness of dancing?! The night before the healing prayer, I sensed the words, "Dance for the healing to come." My Amanda-voice came back with, "But I haven't seen the healing yet. Why would I dance while we're all still broken?" The Prompter of all prompts just smiled back, knowingly, and said, "Dance."

So, out of obedience (by now I was really wondering what kind of Pandora's box I'd opened with the whole "fly like a goose" thing), I drove myself to the church late that Saturday night and stood in our dark, empty sanctuary. I found the spot on the polished floor where the healing prayer would happen the following morning and took off my shoes. God was good enough to provide the music—live jazz from the café next door seeped through the wall. My shoulder stiffly twitched, as I clenched my eyes shut to avoid witnessing my own awkwardness. I don't know what it looked like, but I danced. I pictured the faces of those we would pray over in the morning, and I danced for each one. I felt my muscles begin to loosen, my heart open a crack, my longing leak out, and a little joy shyly emerge. By the end, I was sweating, not because my dance was so exuberant but from the exertion of will it took to override my lament, dancing when I felt like weeping. Psalm 30 expresses it this way: "You turned my wailing into dancing; you removed my sackcloth and clothed me with joy" (v. 11). The psalmist says it in past tense. I was dancing it in future tense.

I danced this lament because I was tired of hesitating, talking, weeping, worrying. I danced it because if I didn't, my heart might break. I don't know the healing God worked in the hearts and bodies of those who came that Sunday, but God asked me to carry a little of it. If I really believed that God would heal these loved ones (whether in this life or the life to come), wouldn't I dance? This is our calling—to be honest about brokenness and, in the same breath, proclaim that brokenness is not the whole story.

We dance not to avoid or numb but to heal our own hearts.

We dance as an act of faith that there are things at work beyond our seeing and understanding.

We dance as testimony to each other and to the world.

How will we know something is happening unless someone is brave enough to say, "Something is happening!"?

I danced for the healing to come for others. As I danced, healing began in me.

Celebrating what God can do without knowing what God will do brought me to a new place of hovering—hovering between the known and the unknown. Paradox is a place where we are very uncomfortable and where God is right at home. Paradox is the realm of God and children. It's a place Jesus visits in the garden of Gethsemane, and his prayer there provides the perfect way for humans to hover. First, he addresses the prayer to a Being for whom all things are possible. Then he honestly confesses his own human desire, that the cup might be removed. Then he closes by saying, "Not my will, but yours be done" (Luke 22:42). There is space in this prayer for God to be God and humans to be human. There is a way for us to be honest about our hope for particular outcomes and at the same time to trust that God is good and powerful regardless of how the prayer is answered. During the healing prayer service, I read the Gethsemane story from Mark and summed it up like this: "We don't know what God will do, but we know what God can do." It's the way to do kingdom things in kingdom ways, childlike things in childlike ways. The very posture of releasing control and risking to ask God for healing, without knowing what he'll do, does itself heal our spiritual alienation. Getting our desired outcomes feels good, but releasing our control to open ourselves to the God we ultimately desire is even better.

Released from Adultishness

On the one hand, I was drawn so powerfully toward something, while on the other, I felt the pain of what it might cost me. Something about these new possibilities held such promise that I was willing to question old, familiar things, things I'd thought were inherent to my true nature. Although I had no idea how to do it, I began to face my Amanda self. God confronted her kindly through the message of a children's book. Antoine de Saint-Exupéry's *The Little Prince* follows a young prince as he travels through space, stopping briefly on tiny planets, each inhabited by just one person. He meets a parade of characters: a king who sees people only as potential subjects to rule, a vain man who sees people only as potential admirers, a drunkard who drinks to forget how ashamed he is (of drinking), a businessman obsessed with accuracy, a lamplighter whose work is never complete, and a geographer who is too important to actually explore the places he maps. After meeting each character, the prince remarks, "Grown-ups are certainly very strange!"[26]

As I took in these strange and tragic characters, my Amanda self smiled with recognition and slowly, sadly resigned herself. In my desperate efforts to play the grown-up, I'd embraced a distorted caricature of adultlikeness: adultishness. Adultishness made me believe that comfort was found in control over others, their admiration of me, my accuracy, my ability to name

"Grown-ups don't look like grown-ups on the inside either. Outside, they're big and thoughtless and they always know what they're doing. Inside, they look just like they always have. Like they did when they were your age. Truth is, there aren't any grown-ups. Not one, in the whole wide world."

Neil Gaiman, *The Ocean at the End of the Lane*

FIELD GUIDE

Which character from *The Little Prince* do you most relate to? What would it look like to live differently?

and manage the world around me, my hyperattention to my responsibilities. And every time it all came crashing down, I, like the drunkard, found ways to numb the pain of it. I'd imagined being an adult meant understanding, fixing, and producing, and these false-self habits had been affirmed by my Western upbringing. But now, through these fictional characters, I saw how grown-ups can be terribly fragile, perhaps *because* of our desperate efforts to be strong. I saw how *I* was terribly fragile. I'd already chosen to be childlike. To do so I had to set aside my adultish, controlling habits.

Jesus is inviting us to be like children in the garden once more. In Eden, those children of God knew their limitations and were unashamed. They weren't surprised or anxious that they needed something beyond themselves. Any sign of something lacking in themselves was simply a sign to reach outside of themselves. Children are not too proud to ask for help, sustenance, comfort. A child's first instinct on being born is to cry out, which is to say, "I don't have something, and I will communicate that need to someone beyond myself." Satan shows the children in the garden both their desired outcome and their inability to achieve it, shaming their inadequacy, telling them they're naked. They'd always been naked, but now they feel a lack in it. In inviting us to be like these children again, God says, "Who told you that you were naked?" (Gen. 3:11). We are called to be children unafraid of what is lacking in ourselves, renaming the nakedness as the opportunity to put on God. A nakedness that is ashamed hides, desperately grabbing at whatever is at hand to cover itself. A childlike nakedness is unashamed and remains open to communion.

When we first explore the garden like children, something within us will fight it with surprising vigor. It's a temptation C. S. Lewis knew: "When I became a man I put away childish things, including the fear of childishness and the desire to be very grown up."[27] That desire to be very grown-up has a spiritual element—one that wants to keep us entirely independent, self-sufficient. It will tell us that "to be taken seriously" is our highest goal. Unlike healthy adultlikeness, this adultishness is a childishness that dresses up in grown-up clothes. Adultishness will keep us always striving for control and good repute. In its fear of powerlessness, adultishness abuses power by overuse. We see this in every tyrannical ruler throughout Scripture. And to find the ultimate example, we need look no further than the Pharisees. Theirs is the worst kind of adultishness, which shapes the ways of God into one more way to retain control. Jesus made it clear what he thought of that.

Adultishness is an expression of our false self. This is language that psychologists and contemplatives have used to describe the ways we, as adults, learn to compromise our own integrity in order to survive. "As we walk out of the garden

"Maybe this is what Jesus meant when he said, 'It is those who become like little children who will enter the Kingdom of God.'" . . . We return to that early childhood, as it were, running naked and exposed into the great room of life and death. . . . God has accepted me in my most naked being, and I can now give it all back to God exactly as it is with conscious loving trust that it will be received. What else would God want?"

Richard Rohr, *The Art of Letting Go*

Figure 2.1. How are you afraid to be powerless? What part of that is healthy and what part is your false, adultish self at work? Is there a way you're sensing an invitation from God to release your control? What might it look like to say yes to that?

of innocence towards the world, we . . . change from an authentic to an inauthentic relationship with our self. . . . As the child becomes more involved with the world they seek to conform and to fit in with what seems normal and conventional."[28] Thomas Merton used the language of the false self to describe our "shadow," which are those parts we try to hide from others (and even ourselves), and our "disguise," the alternate persona we try to show to the world instead.[29] This is helpful language because it reminds us that whatever God calls us to let die is not our actual self but our false self (even though these false selves have been ours so long that at first it seems he is asking us to let our true selves die). Jesus's direction to lose ourselves in order to find ourselves has for centuries been interpreted to mean our physical selves have to die for our spiritual selves to live, creating an unscriptural and unhealthy body/spirit dualism. But instead, Merton's language helps us discover a different way to understand what should die and what should live. As we step into each invitation from the Spirit, each direction from Scripture, the discomfort will likely reveal many false selves—desperate efforts to remain in control, to look good, to gain good repute—and each time we press into these invitations we'll have an opportunity to let the false self die and to watch the true self come alive!

An Invitation to Empty

This decision to forget ourselves on purpose is a daily decision. Our adultish selves keep waking up every morning imagining they're in charge, and every morning we have to remind them of their part in the grand scheme. Everything in our upbringing has taught us that living is about becoming more. Our habit is to always seek to gain—more insight, skills, ideas. But Scripture also talks about losing stuff: vines require pruning to become more fruitful (John 15:2), precious metal must be refined in fire to become pure (Prov. 17:3; 25:4). We like the idea of growing and of shining bright but want to do so without the pain and loss of the pruning shears and the furnace. If we want to become more Christlike, it feels like moving backward to become less. And yet if we want to be more and more like the One who became less, to be more like him is to let go. This is what Scripture tells us: "Have the same mindset as Christ Jesus: Who, being in very nature God, did not consider equality with God something to be used to his own advantage; rather, he made himself nothing by taking the very nature of a servant, being made in human likeness" (Phil. 2:5–7).

I began to wonder if, as God emptied himself of equality with God, setting aside power, he actually became more human than we are. I began to wonder if my self-filling project, as satisfying as it might have seemed, had kept me so full there was little space for God. Seventeenth-century Quaker Isaac Penington wrote this:

> Be no more than God has made you.
> Give over your own willing;
> Give over your own running;
> Give over your own desiring to know or to be anything.
> Sink down to the seed which God sows in the heart.
> Let that grow in you;
> be in you;
> breathe in you;
> act in you;
> And you will find, by sweet experience, that the Lord knows, loves, and owns that and will lead you to the inheritance of life, which is God's portion.[30]

I journaled: "What might it look like if, instead of working to build myself up, I devoted my energy to actively, consciously emptying myself, giving over my own willing, running, desiring? What if all along my efforts to be more have smothered the seed that God has sown in my heart? If I emptied, might it clear the way for that seed to grow, for God's work to take root in me?"

My morning prayers are now often devoted to this work of emptying. It is hard work, but simple. I begin every day with the same confessions about my habits—to look strong, to control, to understand. As I let each problem, each heartache rise to my consciousness, I confess the ways I have been working in my own strength. And then the hardest, but best, prayer comes. To give it over. To say, "I confess the ways I'm trying to fill myself up. To be more than I am. To be you." This is not an effort to avoid action. I don't say "I'm only human" as an excuse. These prayers put things back in order: I am human, God is God. These prayers help me, as the day unfolds, to watch where God is at work and how he calls me, small and human as I am, to respond.

It is excruciating to hand over everything I've been trying to accomplish, every way I've been protecting myself. It goes against my education, my socialization, everything the media has taught me—all my Amanda habits—and it brings me to a bare, open place. When I first visited that place, I was ashamed, ordinary, naked. But over time, the shame gave way to freedom. I became accustomed to the discomfort of my own humanity. Or perhaps I was distracted from the discomfort by the beauty of what I discovered growing there. As I emptied, I cleared away all that had piled up on the seed God had sown in my heart. I removed everything that blocks the light and thwarts the growth. Once I've set aside my own efforts (even my efforts to empty well), I come to that open, quiet place that God knows, a place where I am only human and my need for God is plain. God is the seed God has planted in us. And when we empty ourselves of all our efforts, God can grow in that soil.

I first began this emptying prayer simply as a way to declutter all the junk that poor, anxious, adultish Amanda had hoarded. I had no thought for what might fill the newfound space, only that I had to clear out all my desperate efforts to be more than I am. And the more I emptied, the more new possibilities began to show themselves.

When we can't feel the Holy Spirit's presence we often say, "Fill me with your Spirit." Certainly, Scripture tells us stories of dramatic moments when people were filled with the Spirit for the first time (Acts is full of them), but Scripture also assures us that we have been given the Spirit, a truth that shapes our identity. The Spirit does not come and go but actively, permanently marks us as in Christ. The Spirit's indwelling is a reality for us to live daily, not a goal for us to work toward. I see no verse that says, "If you don't feel the Spirit then ask for the Spirit again." Sure, it's helpful for us to make the choice to invite the Spirit, but without realizing it we've fallen into this habit of imagining the Spirit comes and goes with how much we sense God's power and comfort. It's easy to think that if God has promised us the Spirit but we don't feel the Spirit's power, maybe we're doing something wrong. This reinforces our habit of working harder in our own strength.

What I began to learn was that I'd extended a confusing kind of invitation to the Spirit: "Come and live here but I hope you're okay contorting to fit in the space between the clutter. Most of it is useless junk, but it makes me feel secure, so you'll just have to live with it." Not much of a welcome to a treasured guest! What if the Spirit—never one to coerce—can only really thrive in us if we're willing to clear out the clutter? In most cases this clutter is not a pleasant muddle of knickknacks but a desperate hoarding of broken promises and anxious vows that shape a maze we've confused for home. The emptying can be done. And we may even need the help of the Spirit to do it.

If I was going to follow this childlike instinct that was drawing me toward joy, it's only natural that the parts of me shaped by self-sufficiency might shame the joy. As these child-like instincts drew me toward rest, why would the parts of me addicted to productivity affirm that instinct? When I was led toward play and delight, I shouldn't have been surprised that my desperately sensible self complained that this was just foolish and messy. As that childlikeness called me to empty, whatever parts of me that have been shaped by consumerism and comfort told me that emptying would leave me having nothing, being nothing. To be like a child is to rest in new possibilities, though they seem ridiculous to our adultish selves and to the adultish world around us. To be like a child is to hear all that clamoring around us and to choose, instead, to rest and receive. "In receiving and not grasping, in inheriting and not possessing, in praising and not seizing, [we know] that initiative has passed from our hands and we are safer for it."[31]

What may have begun as whimsy—wandering in the woods, hearing new notes in old songs, watching every sunrise like it was a miracle—catalyzed a radical and terrifying transformation. But I was simply being called toward the things of the kingdom: self-giving, believing in mystery, and partnering with

FIELD GUIDE

I began the practice of emptying prayer first simply to clear out my anxieties and was surprised to find that emptying didn't leave me empty but more available to the Spirit. Practice this prayer with the guided emptying prayer video at www.UnfetteredBook.org/unfettered.

a God who is making all things new. There is nothing strange here, not for folks who claim to be Christians, anyway. But compared to our safe, familiar, adultish, Western ways, childlikeness may cause quite a stir. It may create some real discomfort, even some conflict. And we may have some difficulty setting aside our sad habit of adultishness in favor of the childlike, restless, hopeful Spirit at work in us. It's no small choice. But if what is as stake is our availability for the kingdom, might this not be worth everything?

CHAPTER 3

Receive

As flying like a goose led me into habits from childhood, the childhood habits had me resting in a Reality that was mine not to shape but to receive. I'd tried not to have an agenda on my sabbatical, but even trying not to have an agenda can become an agenda of its own. One thing I'd hoped to bring back with me from this eight-week rest was a mountaintop moment or two, and I'd assumed it would take the form of a new idea or insight. But, to my surprise, the closest thing I had to a mountaintop experience took place on a humble hill and involved no words and very little understanding.

In the middle of an ordinary walk on a breezy hill, the grass beckoned me to lie in it, and I did (with only a little adultish concern that it might be silly or a waste of time). I can't say why but I just knew God was with me. For the first time in years my engagement with him was not so he would fix or explain something. It was enough that we were together. On the top of that grassy hill, I marveled at the blueness of the sky, the perfection of the breeze. The ground beneath me felt so constant—old and yet always changing. I could almost feel each shoot of grass, pressing up out of the earth beneath me. I knew that, deeper still, there was a molten core, and I could almost feel its pulsing. I let the sun warm my face, listened to a lazy bee. Not one bit of that goodness was my doing: I hadn't tended that grass or birthed that bee. And yet it was all willing to welcome and warm me. I opened my eyes to the clouds and wordlessly wondered, "When you made the world, did you think of me here on this day? When you shaped this hill, this sky, did you know I'd look up and ask you this?"

As I described this experience to a friend, with a kind of longing he asked me, "You hear from God all the time, don't you? What's that like?" It was a little odd to admit, "Yeah, I guess I do." Of course, we all hear from God in beauty and Scripture and sleep every day, but I knew he didn't mean only that. He meant something that feels like specific and direct communication with God. In case my willingness to listen to it communicates a clarity I don't actually have, it may help if I describe how I experience it. It is often vague, so I don't even know for sure it is God. We all have an ear inside our heads that hears our own, unspoken thoughts. Occasionally, for me, this ear also hears words, songs, or phrases that didn't emerge

FIELD GUIDE

How would you describe how it feels to hear from God? Don't assume such communication will be verbal. What if it's an emotion, instinct, or bodily experience? How could you describe these experiences even if only in primitive ways? Are there things you're picking up in instinctive ways/places that you don't like to attend to? These instincts don't have to run the show, but what would it look like to welcome them into the conversation?

from my own thinking—a formed thought that I know I didn't form. But whoever did form it is more poetic and more kind than I am. Sometimes it's like there's an eye in my heart that sees emotional images, like an abstract painting made of color and feeling. At other times it's like my stomach has a sense of touch, a Richter scale that picks up tiny tremors. Very few of these things have a direct connection to the rational, linguistic part of me. These metaphors, images, and urges often have to be expressed as tears, walking, doodling, sleeping, or dancing before they can become English language. Once I can explain them in words, I see how important they are, but not before then. We all have these senses and intuitions in unexpected places. But are we attuned to them? And do we trust them? To help ourselves begin to explain our experiences we may have to begin by talking as children do—that is, by naming bodily experience. Children likely will not say "I'm anxious because it's the first day of school" but rather "I have a tickly feeling in my stomach."[1]

What might God be waiting to give us if we could just rest in a reality shaped by him? What significant things might we discover if we forgot ourselves on purpose and joined in the general dance? I still draw on that hilltop possibility that the peace of God's presence is available to us at any time, in any place, and under any circumstance if we will rest in this reality. In how many other ways was I missing his presence, even as I tried to engage it? I needed a new posture even in my study of God.

Imagining Scripture beyond the Baggage of Western Culture

If I'm honest, I have mixed feelings about Scripture. I've experienced its power. But why does that power frequently seem so elusive? Temperamental? It cannot be compelled to move and inspire. It's easy to take that personally. We see how it provides insight for others; we remember the transcendent moments of our past. So we mine Scripture with every tool at our disposal, armed with commentaries, ready to wrestle it until it blesses us. It may be possible that we've wrung the power from it because we come to it with an agenda, forcing it to show its power on our terms and according to our expectations.

I know how to tower over a text. But domination and control are not the way to begin if I want to receive. To overcome my adultish habits of domination, I started by literally changing my posture, literally resting. I found an audio version of the Bible and I stretched out in bed, letting the story of God be spoken over me. I watched where my mind wandered, which words stood out. I paid attention to what was hard to hear and where my heart sang. I memorized phrases to chew on throughout my day. By the time I listened again that night, it had taken on new life because it had been walking around in me all day. What if the power of the Spirit is lying dormant in these ancient words on these ordinary pages? What if we'll never experience that power until we rest from our own? Can we set aside our own

"Since the Reformation, particularly in the West, Christians of all traditions have often tended to think about scripture as a kind of information manual. We tend to read scripture for the facts (to find out what actually happened) and for the rules (to find out what exactly we are supposed to do about what happened). But to read scripture for information only is to risk missing the sense of it all—sense not only as cognitive meaning but also as meaning felt and touched."

Roger Ferlo, *Sensing God: Reading
Scripture with All Our Senses*

efforts long enough to receive? As I approached Scripture with this childlike posture of resting, receiving, and responding, I began to see the kingdom in a new way. (See the appendix for resources for engaging Scripture in new ways.)

Imagining Church beyond the Baggage of Western Culture

This way of resting in the power of Scripture provided a new kind of peace, but I didn't always feel the peace when I watched the church in the world. Almost every week there seemed to be a new headline about a Christian leader burning out, a Christian leader selling out, a Christian leader proclaiming things in Jesus's name that Jesus never said. And with these troubling headlines came endless (but understandable) statistics about young people leaving the church in droves. My newfound awareness of my own false, adultish self made me newly aware of how often the contemporary Western church is mired in adultishness. I despaired to see how the church's communication to the world is so often one of claiming control and certainty. How can we welcome others into a kingdom that Jesus said was accessed through childlikeness if we've forgotten the way ourselves? I despaired for the sake of the church locally and globally. How can we fix it? How can I fix it? In the middle of one of many conversations growing from that despair, a friend threw up his hands and proclaimed, "The church is a whore."[2]

It left me winded, like a kick to the stomach.

I'd started the conversation lamenting the state of the church. Why was I so disturbed that it had come to this?

With each new headline and statistic my despair grew. I wanted to find hope in words, but I had none. Instead, one morning I found myself flipping mindlessly through old magazine photos of the desert, feeling a strange affinity with each empty space, every messy wilderness. After a particularly personal piece of news left me even more disheartened about the state of the church, I found myself reaching for one of these desert photos to begin a drawing. I had no idea what I wanted it to become, just that I wanted to make something to express my despair. I slipped into a kind of meditative state, sweeping my pencil down the page with flowing lines, top to bottom, from the magazine clouds to the magazine parched earth. As they fell, these pleasing pencil teardrop trails began weaving across one another like rain meandering down a window. It was strangely calming to move my hand repeatedly from top to bottom, to let the tears flow, to imagine the tears might flood the land, that even lamenting might bring life.

I hadn't really thought beyond that, just that I was comforted by the rhythm of tracing the rain tears. And as I sat with my desert covered in these paths of tears, I saw something unmistakable move between the lines. I blinked and there she was again, a young woman, dancing. Where the lines crossed, they'd made shapes: a skirt a-twirl, arms akimbo, hair aloft. It was the first hope I'd felt all week, and I rushed for my oil pastels to bring this woman to life. I helped her find fullness— her hair had to be fire from heaven, her dress had to be green with life. When I was done, I knew exactly who she was; she was Ecclesia, dancing for the healing to come. I understood now why I reeled at the declaration of the church as a whore. It's easy to pass by a woman on the street, see her life of prostitution, and give her a label. But "whores" rarely create themselves. "Whore" is what someone is called after someone else has used her.

It's time to confess.[3] If there's some way that the church has become a whore, it's because *we* have sold *her*, *we* have used *her*. We have made her into an army, an institution, a corporation, a factory. We have boxed her in buildings and brands. We have forced her to produce, made her a slave to our ambitions, chained by our agendas.

If the church has become a whore, it's because *we* have sent her whoring.

But it's not who she is. Even as she's abused by our misuse, she remembers her Beloved and longs for him. Given the slightest opportunity to slip free of our slavery, she will run, skirts flying, straight for him. She hasn't forgotten who she is or whose she is.

> Our beautiful Ecclesia is both timeless and childlike, always hoping, dancing into new places, longing for life.
> She is pure and spotless and lovely, knowing she has been made whole.
> She is quietly fearless, humbly courageous.
> She will not force herself on anyone, but her joy is winsome. Her dance is inviting and her laughter has gravity.
> We cannot look away.
> She is a healer, a creator, a comforter, singing new things into being, drawing many into her song.
> She knows pain but it has not made her bitter, poverty has not made her miserly.
> She feeds multitudes—nourishing the broken, sending them out rejoicing.
> She will not be measured or caged but takes on many surprising forms, all true to her nature.
> She is gifted and multilingual.
> Her gracious speech shapes new stories, describing places we long to visit, ways we long to be.
> She is never reduced by giving herself away, never emptied from pouring herself out.
> She is many things brought together, every color woven into a rich fabric, each part with its purpose.
> She is a tree, bearing many kinds of fruit.
> She is a symphony, played on instruments of many timbres.

She is All and she is One, a whole household in one
  Body.
This bride's heart has never turned from her Beloved.
But she is exhausted from being ravished by our egos,
  appetites, and anxieties.
She longs to run free, hair wild, skirts flying, to fulfill
  her calling.

This was the most hope for the church I had ever known. And it wasn't based on circumstances—as far as I knew, no sudden change to the church had taken place—but on a renewed imagination of what God might be doing. For just a moment, I'd rested from my desperate efforts to fix and control the church and had received something from outside of myself. It was childlikeness that had helped me find her and had opened up a renewed vision of who the church actually is and what her fundamental identity is beneath all our abusive adultish efforts. And it is childlikeness that will help us rest from our desperate efforts to conform the church to our own adultish ways. Childlikeness will help us see her. Childlikeness will help us *be* her.[4]

The very process of creating this image (and the dozens more like it that I've made to console me since) helped me practice these new postures of resting, receiving, and responding. The process began with repetitive pencil strokes, slowing my heart and mind to rest, creating a space to breathe and lament. Then the posture moved to one of receptivity—I had made the pencil marks, but there was some new possibility emerging between them that I hadn't formed, like finding faces in the grain of wood. Receptivity made me hopeful, expectant. Receptivity required patience with what I couldn't yet see. And then once I got a glimpse of what was waiting for me there, I leapt into action. I certainly had a part to play, but I was joining, not initiating. I was not only creating a picture of Ecclesia, I was being trained in her way—rest, receive, respond.[5] The bride knows the way of the child, knows the way of the goose, knows the way of the Spirit.

In light of everything we see in ourselves, in the world, in the church, lament makes sense. Dancing doesn't. When we're groaning, how can we dance? If we have to wait until we're filled with joy before we dance, then dancing is rarely possible. But dancing becomes possible when we're dancing for the healing to come—whether healing for one person, or for our timeless Ecclesia, or for the whole planet. What if we're dancing as an act of faith that healing can come in all those places? And what if the dancing itself releases healing? We're not dancing because everything is right; we're dancing to heal our hope that everything is being made right. Not dancing to avoid lament but dancing because we're worn out with crying, thinking, fixing. Dancing not because our hope is fulfilled but dancing to heal our hope. If the healing of all creation is up to us, we have no time to dance. If we're children, invited to receive the kingdom, dancing becomes possible. Even necessary.

Usually when I plan to make art, I come to the page with a plan. I have an image already in my head, and the challenge is to reproduce that in a tangible form—certainly a legitimate way to make art, but not the only way. This new approach assumed there are forces at work beyond mine, asking me to join.

FIELD GUIDE

This contemplative way of finding an image among random lines is a wonderful, hands-on way to practice the postures we are learning. You need no art experience, and you don't have to find what I found. To try this reflective practice, watch the instructional video at www.Unfettered Book.org/unfettered.

It opened my mind to the possibility that individual effort and initiative are not the only ways to begin. What a possibility that the One who spoke all creation into existence is available every moment if I just rest from my own sad efforts long enough to connect to him. What life and creativity and flourishing might be available! I became intensely aware of how much this has been my way in all of my life—initiating then wondering why my efforts fell flat. My habit was: Respond! Respond! Respond! It troubled me to discover how much this was also my posture in my faith. Spiritual disciplines were too often tools to accomplish my agenda. Reading the Bible, praying, sharing the gospel, these ordinary Christian practices had become devices. Childishness says, "It's all up to God so I can be totally passive." Adultishness says, "It's all up to me so I don't need God." There must be a better way than these two extremes.

Imagining Kingdom beyond the Baggage of Western Culture

The 2010 British Petroleum (BP) oil spill in the Gulf of Mexico covered the front pages for months.[6] We worried: How will we shut it off? How will we clean it up? What went largely unnoticed was a small article hidden in the back pages of the newspaper that popped up months later. It was the story of a naturally occurring bacteria that sucked up two hundred thousand tons of that BP oil.[7] While we're often cautioned to avoid bacteria, most bacteria do not cause disease. Bacteria are in the world for a reason; in fact, they make the world habitable, breaking down decomposing matter and releasing nutrients back into the environment. In this massive oil spill crisis, a tiny, largely ignored presence brought renewal to the devastation in a way that human efforts could not.[8]

Oil spills make headlines. There are industrial-scale "oil spills" of different varieties taking place across our country and planet—distrust among people, oppression of the power-less, the wealthy preying on the poor, abuse of the environment, injustice, division, war, violence, unrest. These crises are very real, and they're easy to talk about because we can name and measure them. They're caused by actual politicians, villains, and unethical corporations.

But God has built "bacteria" into the world to suck up "oil spills." The power of art is always at work; a crisis does not stop a song rising in the heart of a musician; in fact, it may prompt it. The power of the family is ever-present; global unrest does not stop a mother from embracing her child; in fact, it may make her want to do it all the more. And I believe that there is another, undervalued, almost immeasurable force that works like bacteria in an oil spill: the kingdom of God.

Every Thursday morning I meet with a group of six women in the basement of our church. We gather in the nursery so that the preschoolers can play, affording their moms the luxury of a few uninterrupted sentences. At some point in the morning, someone is changing a diaper, someone is nursing, someone is cleaning up a spilled cup of juice (or all three at once). And at the same time, someone is asking, "How can I extend welcome to my new neighbors?" or "How can I respond to my in-laws in a way that reflects Jesus?" or "How can God possibly be at work in this mess that is my life/the world?" We laugh and cry and pray and leave there with a better sense of what it means to live like Jesus in our neighborhoods and homes and bodies. No one writes headlines about the things that happen in a church basement. But we're gobbling up the oil spill, one little bacteria at a time.

The Roman Empire would have made front page news. Its political, economic, and military power were unsurpassed. The generals could be named, the walled cities could be measured, the riches could be weighed, the centurions could be numbered. But where is that empire now? Meanwhile, the early church was virtually invisible. It is hard to measure a ragtag bunch of misfits, meeting in homes, eating and praying and serving their neighbors together. Such an immeasurable thing seems impotent. And yet such a relational, human-scale thing is almost impossible to overthrow or contain. This seemingly insignificant movement has outlived that immense Roman Empire. We long to have institutions, power, measurable effects—to be able to name the leader, see the building, count the resources, report the outcomes—but perhaps it's our organic nature that makes the kingdom truly transformative and unstoppable. Historian Alan Kreider calls this the patient ferment of the early Christian movement:

> It was brewing, but not under anyone's control. It was uncoordinated, it was unpredictable, and it seemed unstoppable. The ferment was spontaneous, and it involved ordinary ingredients that at times synergized into a heady brew. The churches grew in many places, taking varied forms. They proliferated because the faith that these fishers and hunters embodied was attractive to people who were dissatisfied with their old cultural and religious habits, who felt pushed to explore new possibilities, and who then encountered Christians who embodied a new manner of life that pulled them toward what the Christians called "rebirth" into a new life. Surprisingly, this happened in a patient manner.[9]

It is tempting to hear this description of the early church and wish we could rediscover that kind of life, to suppose that kind of energy and growth was a thing just for the early days of the Christian movement. But in the places where the church is growing fastest, Christians still see this kind of patient ferment at work. For example, the *Christian Post* carried an article with the following headline: "'Fastest-Growing Church' Has No Buildings, No Central Leadership, and Is Mostly Led by Women." It went on to describe the way that ordinary, broken people in Iran are leading movements in spite of great persecution, simply by sharing their stories of Jesus.[10]

"Organic" has become a catchword in recent years to describe new (old?) ways of doing church. To some it's code for unprofessional or disorganized. But organic things certainly have structure and bear fruit—it's mysterious to us because the structure defies our efforts to predict or control it. A better word for what we are is "relational." This whole Jesus movement began without headquarters, a corporate structure, or a business plan. Yet it not only survived, it has flourished (and continues to flourish) through war, persecution, even conflict among believers. Every way it has survived and flourished is connected to every way it's not housed in a big, bulky institution. The kingdom has survived because of where it exists: in human hearts, in the relationship between God and human, and between one human and another. It requires no institution for God to do his work in a willing heart, and it requires no institution for us to connect with those around us. Instead, this Spirit of the living God looks for every chance to move, flourishes where there is opportunity, redirects where there is not. And every place the Spirit fills becomes our beautiful Ecclesia, dancing on unhindered—welcoming, nourishing, and healing.

Jesus said the kingdom is like yeast. He promised his way was small, almost undetectable, but working powerfully in every place, in a million tiny ways that come together to make a huge difference. I've never thought, "I'd really like to be part of something that's been compared to yeast." Yeast is tiny, ordinary, unimportant. But imagine for a moment that you have a lump of flour, oil, and water that you absolutely don't want to rise. How would you feel to discover someone had kneaded in a tiny pinch of yeast? How could you ever distinguish between the flour and yeast in order to remove it? The kingdom of God is that tenacious force, ever multiplying, "tainting" death with life. Jesus promised that while his kingdom may not overthrow human empires, it would bring a deeper, less measurable, more transcendent hope—a force that would overcome oppression one heart at a time, heal brokenness one relationship at a time. This Kingdom is the naturally occurring bacteria in every biome, ready to gobble up oil spills one tiny drop at a time.

We can enter into that creative, healing force only if we set aside our habit of shaping reality in our own image. We certainly have an active part to play. But jumping into responsive activity should not be our first move. We should begin with resting and receiving. When we stop striving and begin to pay attention, we'll discover a new momentum at work, drawing us into the gravitational pull of "All Things Made New." In our old habits, rest is a risk—if we stop running the world, the world will stop running. In our old habits, rest is worthwhile only as much as it makes us more productive when we return to our work of running the world. But when the rest allows us to set aside our control and agenda, we receive an entirely new agenda, a better, bigger vision. And the rest allows us to pay attention to the Spirit alive within us, a living entity, always imagining, moving, drawing all into its orbit. And so this thing we receive when we rest from our perceived responsibility for the world will give us a taste of something new. It will awaken new hungers in us, make us long for every taste of it, send us scattering the seeds of this fruit wherever we go. We'll come to the table and we'll invite others to pull up a chair because we've tasted the fruit and we can't keep it to ourselves. All this resting and receiving will fill us with new things we *have* to share. It will make us want to do something.

You are one small piece of something beautiful and active and powerful. Don't be overcome by the size of the task at hand. It's not yours alone. Ecclesia is alive, the Spirit is at work, the kingdom is at hand. It always has been. It always will be. And you have a part to play.

FIELD GUIDE

When we see so much war, injustice, suffering, and violence, it's hard to believe God is making all things new. As a way to practice the posture of paying attention to what God is making new, my church community created the "All Things New Fest." We simply asked, "What do you do when you believe God is making all things new? Or what do you do to help you believe God is making all things new?" Then we planned a day to get together and share those things. We met in a barn in a big field on a Saturday afternoon, and people set up their expressions of hope. It became an art show, a drumming circle, a prayer tent, a seed bomb-making workshop, a communal painting project, a Hula-Hooping area, a picnic (complete with pop-up Communion—we'd provided bread and wine to be brought out and shared at the right time) and, finally, a barn dance (see the video at www.UnfetteredBook.org/unfettered). Without having to make a big production that costs a lot of money or takes a lot of time, what might your family or community create from asking those same questions? What do you do when you believe God is making all things new? What helps you believe it? Do those things!

CHAPTER 4

What Doesn't
Get in the Way
of Receiving

Once we get out of the habits that have kept us independent from God, receiving is inevitable. In John 15, Jesus
describes a relationship of restful dependence when he invites
us to abide in him as branches abide in their vine. It makes
perfect sense that the branches that are removed from the vine
wither and die and those that remain connected continue to flow
with sap and burst with life. Hildegard of Bingen, the medi-
eval abbess, theologian, naturalist, and doctor, created a word
for this: *viriditas* (sometimes translated as "greening power").
Combining the Latin words for "green" and "truth," this word
describes a reality so much bigger than a statement of fact. The
truth of God's very being is what makes our life and flourishing
possible—physically, emotionally, and spiritually. Jesus's vine
image may be a metaphor but the life force that bears fruit in us

is no less real; it is just harder to see and measure. Hildegard's understanding of life in God is also why she calls sin "drying up." If we choose to separate ourselves from the source of life, it's only natural that we'll wither like those branches snapped off the vine.[1]

We'll be tempted every day to let our anxieties drive us to independence. We'll feel our smallness and be tempted to fix ourselves. Every morning, every meeting, every anxious moment is a choice to either fill ourselves up or to empty. And every time we choose him once more, we'll have a chance to rest in him. And once we rest in God, we can't help but receive from him in some form or other, as surely as "greening power" flows from vine to branch to fruit. The more we do it, the more his power and presence become less abstract and the choice to rest in him becomes a new habit. When we don't feel we're receiving, it may be a sign we still need to release our habits of self-sufficiency. And it's also possible that the greatest way we need to rest is from even our expectations.

FIELD GUIDE

1. If it's hard to trust that God's life force is really at work, pay attention to the power of life that makes a seed sprout, a fetus grow. Reflect on a scar or a way you've watched physical healing in your own body or the body of someone you love. Remember a time when a project flourished, when creative energy and ideas seemingly came from nowhere. Recall a time when healing has come in a relationship between two people. How can these very real examples of life be a visible expression of things just as powerful yet unseen? How could that healing, creative force also be at work in other ways—in us personally and in the church? How do you feel dried up, parched of life? Are there ways that that part of your life has

been separated from the source of life? Invite the Lord to show you where he's inviting you to reconnect to him as the source of all you need.

2. When was the last time you did absolutely nothing? How did you feel about it? There's nothing like stepping out of Western culture's productivity mill to convince us how much we're wrapped up in its lies that our identity is based on our achievements and that rest is self-indulgence. Make time to do absolutely nothing on a regular basis and, while you're doing so, remind yourself, "I'm no use to anyone right now, and yet God delights in me!"

3. What are your expectations of receiving from God? Does it have to look as it has in the past or as it has for others? As you rest, what does it look like to set aside your expectations and just receive whatever God has for you, even if it's not what you'd choose? Sometimes in rest we receive insight, images, prompts, words of encouragement, Scripture, songs, mountaintop moments—obvious experiences of God's presence. And sometimes we receive sleep or tears or even silence, all of which are gifts from God.

4. What if there are miracles happening every moment, and we're just out of touch with them? Have you ever considered the miracle of your own heart, beating away faithfully in your chest? What if the variety of flavors, colors, and textures in your refrigerator (and the fact that someone else grew them, harvested them, and transported them from all over the place) is a miracle? Maybe your pet's affection is a miracle? Or maybe it's a miracle that there are sounds in the world and that we have two built-in sensors on the sides of our head specifically made to receive those sounds? Open yourself to the ordinary miracles that are no less wonderful because they happen every day.

5. If you're having trouble resting, put your body in the hands of something more powerful and rest in that. Float on a body of water. Let yourself be lost in music or a crowd. Sit high in a tree. Lie on the ground; roll down a hill. Rest in things bigger than you. And know they're made by One who is bigger still.

CHAPTER 5

Respond

Following your childlike heart works when you have time off work. For eight weeks with nothing else to do, it had looked like this:

1. Rest (and enjoy the wonders of creation)
2. Receive (whatever peace, wisdom, or direction God offers you in the rest)
3. Respond (by lying in the grass / savoring that cheese)

Sometimes that response led me to a feeling of God's presence or new insights. Often it just helped me be okay in the world as a human. It often was kinder to me than I'd ever been to myself: inviting and calming and slowing. I see now that's one reason why I trusted that the invitation to rest was from God—it couldn't have been only my inner voice because my voice says, "Work more" and "Obsess over every detail." I don't have the patience or wisdom or warmth of these instincts.

When I returned to my normal routine, this whole flying-like-a-goose thing took on more intensity. Not only had those childlike instincts become more accustomed to being given a hearing in my decision making, their prompts became more serious and saying yes to them became more daunting. Soon after I returned to work, our university church found itself in the middle of a campus and neighborhood in crisis.[1] Just a few streets from the church, Samuel Dubose, an unarmed African American man, was shot and killed by a campus police officer during a routine traffic stop. On the day of the hearing for the officer accused of killing him, the university closed its campus out of concern for riots. The whole noisy, urban community of forty thousand students suddenly was unnervingly quiet. Will justice be served? Will there be unrest in our streets? I have to admit that I felt like a child. I knew our church and café should do something, but I had no idea what. I didn't know how it felt to be a person of color in our community that day. I didn't know the best way to foster community-building with police officers or offer real peace to troubled students. I felt foolish and small. I was tempted to host a big event to help the church look like the professional people-helpers and tension-calmers we're supposed to be. But this situation was beyond me, so I did all I could think to do: I called a few folks and said, "What should we do?" All we knew was that we wanted to be there—in the middle of a campus shutdown, where anyone who could had fled to the suburbs, we knew we needed to keep the doors of our church and café open as a sanctuary.

As the time of the press conference drew near, we still had no concrete plans except to keep the building open all night, not knowing what to expect. Would there be riots? Would we be thrown into the middle of chaos? Would we look like fools because nobody turned up? It felt inadequate to have such an un-structured response. If Jesus is supposed to be powerful shouldn't Christians do something "significant" in a crisis? But our simple choice to open a space and put on the coffee became something beautiful. Marchers and healers, church members and neighbors, gathered and made the night whatever it would become. One café regular played hymns on the piano, an intern set up prayer candles, a few brought art supplies, someone made a prayer-journaling table. And throughout the night around seventy-five folks talked about their pain and prayed for peace—all seemingly small things. Not only was I learning to be less ashamed of small things, I was beginning to imagine that small things might save us all. But we might have to be like children, comfortable in our own smallness, to receive that salvation. Like children we invited others because we knew we couldn't do it alone. Like children we asked questions and we listened—to one another and to the Spirit. We didn't feel powerful, but we got to watch a power at work. There's something real about this childlikeness.

But this was only the beginning of trusting my instincts in a new way. In an unhealthy friendship, as I begged for resolution, I sensed a surprising prompt, "She's already moved on; it's okay to step back for now." On a busy street, I had a strange prompt, "Engage with that person you'd rather avoid." In my writing and preaching, I was prompted to share things that made me uncomfortable. As I kept heeding the kind prompts toward rest that I'd known on my sabbatical, the prompts were now guiding me to act and speak in ways that went against my usual, comfortable habits—to give space when I'd rather fix a relationship now, to engage a stranger I'd rather avoid, to raise issues that made people roll their eyes. I could no longer tell the place where my own childlike instincts ended and the Spirit of God began.

Knowing Our Need

It was around this time a crusty old word began to surface in my prayers: revival. As a writer and speaker, I want fresh words. So why did I suddenly feel the need to say "revival"? To write "revival"? Is it possible that if I followed the prompt and said it, I'd discover that others were also longing for it and I wouldn't feel so foolish? It took only one social media post to get serious (virtual) eye rolls from friends—"Really? Aren't we over that? Doesn't that come with extremism and lead to spiritual consumerism?" The shame Amanda had warned me about was becoming a reality, but I was wiser now and knew how to listen to the place in me that couldn't stop saying and praying the word "revival." And I knew that it did not mean some kind of one-off tent meeting that manipulates people into an emotional experience, nor did it mean drumming up a show so we can point to proof of our success. I knew revival meant a change in the hearts of human beings to draw us back to God and his mission. I knew revival meant that in times that seem desperate, when we feel our cultural power slipping, we finally stop grasping for it and turn to our true source of power. Revival does not mean more of the same adultish maneuvering but rather the revival of our ability to receive the kingdom as children.

A longing for this kind of revival led me to write down what I was feeling, partly because I felt foolish and alone and I needed to see if anyone else out there was feeling it too. And partly

FIELD GUIDE

How do you respond to the word "revival"? What's your history with the word? Is there a way you long for something to be revived? In yourself? In the church? In the world? What would that look like? What would it take to let yourself long or hope for it? What holds you back?

How might your despair be connected to your desire for revival?

because my longing threatened to break me into pieces if I held it in. My words tumbled out in this form.[2]

> There's a word I'm hearing a lot from Christians: "Desperate."
> I'm hearing it from church planters who have watched too many plants wither.
> I'm hearing it from Christian colleges, as their classes dwindle.
> I'm hearing it from Christian writers, navigating culture wars.
> I'm hearing it from Christians whose hearts are broken over poverty, racism, human trafficking, violence.
> From Christians who are noticing their congregations shrinking, their cultural voice fading.
> It's no wonder we're feeling desperate!
> The good news is that desperation holds immense potential if we have the right response.

As we feel the upheaval of everything in the church and the world, we react as adults, accustomed to the habit of taking action. As we feel the limitations of our power, we scramble for new ways to make a difference, new ways to prop up our crumbling congregations, our crumbling hopes. But it's not working. And we're worn out. What if we were to let the desperation change us? Romans 8:15 says, "For you did not receive a spirit of slavery to fall back into fear, but you have received a spirit of adoption. When we cry, 'Abba! Father!' it is that very Spirit bearing witness with our spirit that we are children of God" (NRSV).

God has certainly entrusted us with his church. And we've taken on full responsibility for it for so long that we've forgotten whose it is. When our efforts fail, we just try something else. We live in fear of letting God down, working like slaves, shouldering this task alone. What would it look like to feel the desperation, not as slaves but as children? If you're a slave and you feel overburdened, you resent your master and work harder for fear of ramifications. If you're a child and you feel overburdened, you do the only thing a child can do: you cry out to your father. Children often don't even know what to ask for; they just know whom to turn to. So, maybe what we most need is simply to cry, "Abba! Father!"

"Abba" is found only three times in the New Testament, but in every case it is not a word said *about* God but a word said *to* God. It is cried out by those who know their dependence on him, who know how to trust his goodness and provision. We need to say "Abba!" because things are getting desperate.

Our most pressing problem right now is not to "fix" our brokenness on issues of sexuality or the shrinking church or even racism and poverty (as important as all those are). Our most pressing problem is our belief that the burden of fixing is entirely ours. This is not a belief we often admit but a belief we regularly live. What if we stopped our slavish, fearful striving long enough to remember we're not slaves and to cry out like children to our Father? It may not provide an instant, obvious fix to the pressing problems of the church and the world, but it could bring a different, better solution—even renewal. Marva Dawn proposes a hopeful possibility: "I believe this could be a time of revival if we let weakness be the agent for God's tabernacling."[3]

When we cry, "Abba! Father!" his Spirit testifies to our spirits that we are indeed his children. His Spirit reminds us that we are not alone, that our world is his, our work is his, that his Spirit is striving with our spirits, longing with our spirits. Revival is not measured in new buildings or programs or book sales or conferences (although sometimes true revival sparks such things). Revival is measured in hearts turned to him.

And so, as humbling and uncomfortable but surprisingly simple as this may seem:

> Revival begins when God's people acknowledge their need for him.
>
> Revival begins when human hearts remember how to cry, "Abba! Father!"
>
> Revival is inevitable when we learn to receive the kingdom like children.

There's a wonderful possibility hidden in this very desperation that we fear is our undoing. But only if we let it teach us our need for him.

As I shared this possibility in the article I wrote, I found I never cared more about the response I might get to a piece of writing. I needed to know I was not alone in my despairing or in my hoping. But if I was looking for friends in my longing for revival (revival, after all, usually implies change to a community), I was out of luck. Instead of solidarity, there was only the lonely sound of crickets. And still that "R" word would not leave me alone. It just kept working its way into my conversations and journal and prayers.

This is what I wrote in one journal entry:

> God gives me a tiny seed—a hope, a whisper, a glimpse, a sense, a promise.
>
> He asks me to take it and steward it.

"Why does the kingdom of God belong to little children? Apparently just because they need it."

Judith M. Gundry, *The Child in the Bible*

The beauty of its hidden potential overwhelms me.

The questions it raises awake my curiosity.

I want to see, to understand.

Why has he given me this seed?

So I can tell others? But I don't know enough.

So I can make it grow?

So I can celebrate when it grows?

I hold the seed but I hunger for the fruit.

The closest way to get fruit from a seed is to suck the
    seed—try to taste any remnant.

But seeds don't grow in mouths.

Shall I dissect the seed? But wouldn't that kill it?

Give me the patience to sow the seed—even in soil that
    seems rotting—what fertile soil it will become!

Mine is not to be the sun or the rain, to burst the germ or
    bring forth the shoot.

Mine is to tend, to watch, to wait, to be ready when it
    breaks through!

I know now that I was being taught to overcome my desire
to be liked and comfortable and understood. This was prepa-
ration for the prompts yet to come, because this Bible I claim
to follow asks me to do and say things that look weird. In the

FIELD GUIDE

How have you seen or experienced power abuse by Christians? How
have you been guilty of it? What baggage do you carry from previous
experiences of church or Western Christianity?

early church, Christian ways were countercultural in a folksy, peculiar way. These days, after centuries of Christian power, Christian ways have become countercultural in a way that can be threatening. In many places our ways have become practices of colonization, weapons to force our perspective, tools to manipulate others. To find a Christian way forward with all that history, we have to wrestle with a lot of baggage—our own and the church's.

If the church is a family, it's an old family with a lot of baggage. It's easy, in any family, to let our choices be shaped by the baggage as we try to avoid the extremes of our history. But if we're reactionary, we end up setting aside the way Scripture defines our mission, as we throw out many babies with much bathwater. If we're not careful, we find ourselves living in the negative space left between the baggage, defined by reaction to the extremes of the past. So as uncomfortable as it was, I chose to say yes to some deeply scriptural (and, at the same time, deeply countercultural) things, to watch how they might be redeemed. The earlier prompt to obey the instruction in James 5:14 to pray for healing had showed me not only how hard this would be but also that I would survive it. So as Scripture revealed more and more ancient Christian practices we've shied away from, our community committed to reimagining them. Together we named the discomfort of pressing into things that we've seen abused (and that we've abused) to find the true seed in each thing again.

Imagining Christian Language beyond the Baggage of Western Culture

Childlike wonder had opened up new insights in the pages of Scripture. And these ancient words still had surprising power. They reminded me that Christians used to speak in striking ways about God, as if God is actually engaged in our daily lives. Without meaning to, I'd long since become rather post-Christian in my own language. I'd been turned off by the twisted messages of a prosperity gospel, so I'd stopped thanking God for his provision. I'd been manipulated one time too many by someone telling me God's will for me and disappointed one time too many by God not telling me his will for me, so I had just stopped crediting him, stopped listening for him. But if Scripture is about anything, it's about moment by moment reliance on the Spirit of God, trusting that every good and perfect gift is from him, that he is with us in suffering, that his Spirit guides and comforts us. And this awakening child in me had little patience for safety or cynicism. So with that child's urging, I made a commitment to talk as if God is at work. I soon learned how uncomfortable it felt to say "Praise God!" or "I sense God . . ." But together our community chose to press into the discomfort, to find humble ways to express certainty in God even as we felt uncertain. The more we said the "weird" things, the more we remembered how much we need to hear them.

Imagining Spiritual Warfare beyond the Baggage of Western Culture

As we were getting used to the discomfort of that scriptural prompting, soon we began to notice how much Scripture talks about spiritual forces. But genuinely biblical language about dark forces now brings to mind cartoon devils and low-budget horror movies and deliverance ministry radio programs from the 1980s. We don't want to sound like everything in life is explained by angels or demons, and we'd rather not smack of the Middle Ages (or a Frank Peretti book). But Scripture talks of a very real battle with very real victims and very real victories. So while it felt a bit like a script from a bad movie, we began to learn how to call out forces that oppose us, as little as we understand their efforts. We didn't need to fully understand or to feel powerful. We could embrace our own limitations and say, "If there are any forces at work here that are telling lies, undermining, tempting, accusing, or bringing confusion or dissension, we speak against them in Jesus's name." We began to simply claim the power of Jesus. We began to rediscover the power of his name from watching the power it has over forces we can't see.

Imagining Authority beyond the Baggage of Western Culture

Spiritual warfare made us more aware of how much Scripture talks about authority, and not only over dark forces. We may think first of Jesus's humility, but Scripture also describes his astounding authority. Although we rarely see it at work these days, there is a kind of self-emptying authority in the Bible, even though this may seem like one more awkward thing for us to reimagine in light of our Western Christian heritage of domination. It's a strange time to begin testing this kind of authority—right when Christians are particularly sensitive to how power is often abused. To tentatively step out to act and speak with authority in the contemporary church is often to be put in your place, to be told, "Leadership has been abused. We don't do leadership anymore." But Jesus led with authority. And Jesus developed leaders. He just defined authority differently. His authority came from how much he emptied and served. He had the right to speak because of how much he had released, setting aside his own agendas and giving his whole self. When we take a rest from our own authority, we receive a different kind of authority. And it calls us to respond. The way I was feeling called to respond was making me more and more uncomfortable. But I couldn't set it aside.

Imagining the Second Coming beyond the Baggage of Western Culture

This new capacity for discomfort led into even more discomfort, talking as if Jesus is actually coming again. The New Testament tells us to be alert, stay awake. Instead, we're dozy. We're embarrassed that we keep waiting for him, and he still hasn't arrived. On the one hand, Scripture tells us about the remarkable signs of Jesus's return. On the other hand, it says no one knows when (including Jesus!) and that life will be going on as usual. It can be true both that life is going on as usual and that strange signs are taking place. Do we need to know exact moments, make a science of measuring every sign in order to long for the Lord's return? Can we bear to be like a child on Christmas Eve, even if it feels like Christmas morning never comes?

I had thought I was pretty invested in my faith. I was familiar with the scriptural concept that it might cost me my comfort. But this was a level of social discomfort that was entirely new. Choosing to pray for healing and against dark forces, to talk with Christlike authority about revival and end times and mystery will quickly make you a pariah even among Christians. The only way I've found to get over the discomfort is to name the discomfort and do it anyway.

Why would I keep doing these awkward, painful, embarrassing things? Any time I wanted I could have just stopped. But I'd had a glimpse of something small and real that drew me closer. By now I'd had a year's practice following the draw of small things—at first, in the form of picket fences and hilltop breezes. They'd taught me that small things might hold great mysteries. Back then most of the conflict and discomfort was within my own self—choosing to trust that "insubstantial" things might reveal Reality. But now this attention to small things was beginning to cost me relational and social comfort.

For a people-pleaser, that is real death. And for a safety-keeper, it is real death. I was feeling those deaths and yet I couldn't stop. For some reason, to gain whatever I'd caught a glimpse of, I was willing to go against my own self-preservation. I was willing to be in conflict with people I love; I was willing to make mistakes; I was willing to look awkward, be uncomfortable. I was willing to sell everything for a tiny pearl. This kingdom might cost us everything! But once we begin to see the surprising

FIELD GUIDE

1. Are you hesitant to use Christian language like "Praise God" or "I sense God"? Why? What has been your experience with language like this? What would it look like to do the scriptural things without the cultural baggage? To use kingdom language in kingdom ways again?

2. Are you hesitant to talk about or pray against spiritual forces? Why? What has been your experience? What would it look like to do the scriptural things without the cultural baggage? To proclaim kingdom power against darkness in kingdom ways again?

3. Are you hesitant to talk about or step into your authority? Or maybe you're hesitant to follow someone who talks about or steps into their authority? Why? What has been your experience? What would it look like to do the scriptural things without the cultural baggage? To use kingdom authority in kingdom ways again?

4. Are you hesitant to talk about or long for Jesus's return? Why? What has been your experience? What would it look like to do the scriptural things without the cultural baggage? To do kingdom things in kingdom ways again?

power of small things, we can't look away. A tiny crack in what we think is reality lets in beams of such overwhelming joy that we will dig with our bare hands past all we thought was real to find what is truly real.

When we choose to do kingdom things in kingdom ways, we're forced to discern exactly how each thing has been abused and what is worth keeping. It hones something in our language, our understanding, ourselves. It releases us from empire. This honing made me more humble and more honest about my longings. Knowing we need something beyond ourselves and being willing to long for it means living in mess and incompleteness, everything our adultish selves strive to avoid. I'm still not comfortable with humility or longing or mess, but I'm getting used to the discomfort.

Redeemed by Obedience

While I thought I was redeeming these ancient practices and language, this experiment soon began redeeming me. My heart grew a new capacity to hold both mystery and certainty. In times past, I had abused these scriptural practices by engaging in them with the wrong kind of certainty: claiming to know precisely what is happening in the spiritual realm. And when I didn't have that kind of certainty, I demanded it of God and told him he was mean when he denied it to me. When he didn't act on my timeline, I wondered if he really existed. In the past, my discovery of my abuse of ancient practices had led me to give up the practices altogether. Neglect is just a different kind of abuse. Now to take them back up again in all their mess and mystery I needed language to sum up Jesus's faithful courage in Gethsemane: I don't know what God will do but I know what he can do. I began to discover how to communicate certainty about the things I'm supposed to be certain about while leaving room for the things that are supposed to be mysterious.

"Life is hard. AND God is good. Somehow."

"I'm sensing this from God. Does it resonate with you?"

"In this world we will have trouble. AND Jesus has overcome this world."

"We don't know exactly what darkness is doing, but we know it has no place here. We know the name of Jesus is greater."

"God is making all things new."

"Come, Lord Jesus!"

It allowed a childlike confidence without a need for adultish certainty in the details. It opened the possibility for a new kind of resting that invited me to set aside my own control and that allowed for a new kind of receiving. It taught me that it's possible to do kingdom things in kingdom ways again.

The world is old and the church with it. Everything has been hashed over so many times and every practice has been twisted for so long that we've lost the freshness of what Jesus actually offers us. We can't hear "kingdom" without remembering the abuses of every despot through the centuries. We can't hear "Spirit" without imagining the ravings of fanatics. But we need the kingdom and the Spirit—what they actually are—more than ever. Whatever version of Christianity we say we're over is not the true Christian faith. I still long for a place where God reigns, and I still need the Spirit's power. My friend Leonard

"The task of prophetic imagination and ministry is to bring to public expression those very hopes and yearnings that have been denied so long and suppressed so deeply that we no longer know they are there."

Walter Brueggemann, *The Prophetic Imagination*

Allen sums this up succinctly: "Without the Spirit's power, discipleship gets tamed or toned down to what seems humanly possible, simply reasonable, and culturally appropriate. After Christendom that isn't enough."[4]

What if those childlike prompts in me were a place where the Spirit had been working all along? I could no longer tell the difference between my own childlike wonder and the promptings of the Spirit. What if these instincts that prompted speech and action were a natural connection to God at work in me? It was surprising how the more I continued my practices of rest, every day I knew a gift to be shared or a prayer to be prayed or a note of encouragement to be sent. I didn't always understand a prompt, and so I often added my own "so that" or "because": give to that person in need (so that I can single-handedly solve their poverty), encourage that stranger (so that he'll start attending my church), write that article (so that lots of people will read it). But that had me making grand claims about outcomes that I desired. So I learned to keep the prompts primitive—what had I *actually* been prompted to do? I made a commitment that I would always say yes to the prompts if my only hesitation was my own discomfort. This was a dangerous promise to make—and one that would stretch me more than I could have imagined.

Here's why this is important: the things I felt called to say and do weren't for my own sake. I felt led to pray for healing

---

FIELD GUIDE

How have you added your own interpretation to prompts or made assumptions about reasons or outcomes? What would it look like to keep them primitive?

---

for people who seemed beyond hope, to long for the renewal of the church, to trust that God was truly making all things new. It felt like it would break me to hold in my human body both the pain of what is and the imagination of what can be. I began to understand why folks thought the prophets were crazy: lamenting when all was rosy and dancing when all was in ruins. God asked them to carry his imagination for what he could and would do. My imagination was as broken as my heart, so why would I keep telling myself to dance for healing to come? Why would I keep sensing assurances that this story wasn't a tragedy but rather just wasn't finished yet? It had to be God's imagination I was being asked to carry because all I had was despair—my hurting friends would never see healing, the church had burned its bridges, the world was irreparably broken. Why wasn't God quelling the violence, healing the distress, providing for those in poverty, restoring families and cities, establishing justice? How could I trust that his promises were true when the world was only brokenness?

Productive Pain

On a particularly painful day, my morning walk had me feeling Romans 8:22–23 in my body: "We know that the whole creation has been groaning in labor pains until now; and not only the creation, but we ourselves, who have the first fruits of the Spirit, groan inwardly while we wait for adoption, the redemption of our bodies" (NRSV). As the memory of my own labor pain wracked my spirit, I heard the surprising question: "What if all the world's pain is labor pain?" With the suggestion came an image I would never have created, not only because it was a little surreal but also out of fear of heresy—an image of God giving birth. There was no distraction about God's gender, no need to figure out what body part God might need to give birth, because God was light and the source of all life and it was perfectly reasonable to imagine God experiencing both the joy and the pain of bringing life to the world. And in this beautiful upheaval, God cried out, "Behold, I make all things new!"

My heart had been only hollowness. I had no creative energy to imagine such a transcendent possibility. It was a gift that sent me straight home, where I opened up my laptop and wrote a piece I called "A Memo to Languishing Prophets" (as much to myself as to anyone else).

My dear, disillusioned ones,
I see what you want for the world.
I love how you care.
When folks ask how you are, you answer in big ways:
How your heart breaks for the brokenness,
How your spirit longs for all that is missing.
You want to see healing but it's never enough.

May I remind you of your childlike self?
How you dealt with the depth of emotion?
You weren't crippled by the two sides of your
    experience.
You found joy even as you waited for joy,
Signs of change, even as you waited for change.
You weren't afraid to live into things you didn't yet see,
Weren't ashamed to cry or dance.
Weren't too proud to say aloud, "I hope . . ."

I love how you reach to draw heaven to earth,
Strain to bring healing, to see life and wholeness and
    beauty.

But it's never enough, is it?

You know the story:
In this life you will not see heaven in its fullness.
But you will see miracles.
Even in a greedy world
There are people still giving.

In an anxious world
There are people still trusting.
It defies logic that in ugliness there is any sign of
    beauty,
In hate there is any sign of hope,
In chaos there is any sign of order.
Someone is planting a garden in desolation.
Someone is painting in a war zone.
Someone is dancing in the ruins.
Someone is making a feast in scarcity.

It's a miracle that, thousands of years after Jesus,
There are people still preaching about him,
Still waiting for him.

Even as you lament the dimness of the light,
Fan into flame any flicker you see.
Even as you lament the smallness of the choir,
Begin the song, feeble though it may be.

Keep seeing all that is lacking
But don't let it blind you to all that is growing.
Don't let your desire for more heaven
Make you languish.
Don't let all that is missing
Make you believe that I am not at work.

Do you think that you love and long more than I do?

Here is my best work:
To call you now to action.
Not because you feel great
But because the longing in you is my longing.
Not because you know exactly how to act
But because I am already at work.

I don't send you out alone.

But it may feel like it.

I call you to dance where there is desperate seriousness.
I call you to break into song where there is despair.
I call you to discomfit those who have surrounded
themselves with all good things.
I call you to comfort those who have nothing.

Read the prophets.
Remember how strange they were:
Performance artists, speaking words of peace in war,
words of challenge in false peace.
I called them to do ridiculous things.
They didn't want to do them.
But from them the people saw that something was at
work,
Something that defied logic, something wondrous and
terrifying.

You are waiting to see dancing and singing and
disruption?
Perhaps you are the one to begin it.
Then all who are waiting will see it.
In you.
You will feel alone.
You will feel strange and awkward and self-conscious.
But you are not alone.
If you will begin it you will see how many are waiting.
And as others join in your dancing and singing and
speaking and working,
You will see what has been true all along:
That I began the dance and the song.
That I am at work in this world.

Your part is to let your body express what your heart
aches to see,
Let it take on human flesh.
And as you see what you're longing to see,
It will fulfill the longing in me.[5]

FIELD GUIDE

How do you carry both lament and hope at the same time? How does it feel it might break you? Which do you carry most naturally? How could you add the other without losing the first?

How might your longing be something good wanting to get out of you? How could the longing become a piece of art, an act of goodness, a message of hope?

CHAPTER 6

What Keeps Us from Responding

Unless you become like a child, Jesus said, you will never enter the Kingdom of Heaven, and maybe part of what that means is that in the long run what is good about religion is playing the way a child plays at being grown up until he finds that being grown up is just another way of playing and thereby starts to grow up himself. Maybe what is good about religion is playing that the Kingdom will come, until—in the joy of your playing, the hope and rhythm and comradeship and poignance and mystery of it—you start to see that the playing is itself the first-fruits of the Kingdom's coming and of God's presence within us and among us.

—Frederick Buechner, *Now and Then:*
A Memoir of Vocation

What began as rest was now calling me to action. But now something new in me resisted. When you start talking about the Spirit there are all kinds of easy stereotypes—emotional, subjective, outsider stereotypes. We live our lives trying to manage others' perceptions of us and our perceptions of ourselves. Rarely do we even name the caricatures that constrain us, silently working not to be that person in our family, that stereotype that hovers in the culture. But, as I came to discover, the Spirit dances on with little regard for such small, sad categories. Too often we define ourselves negatively, working hard to avoid being something, letting ourselves be shaped by the space left between, the result of which is a contorted identity.

Here's where the dancing prompt took on new meaning. Dancing had become a way to deal with the angst of feeling called to do things I didn't really want to do. I'd learned that dancing is the kind of thing prophets do when nothing makes sense. While dancing out that angst one morning, I saw how many caricatures I work to avoid: one clumsy move means I'm a socially awkward person. A hip jiggle means I'm an immodest woman. My heart's openness to the music means I'm an emotionally unstable person. My abandon to the dance makes me a childish person.

As the music ended, I remembered how I watched my children dance when they were small. No thought was given—by me or by them—to how coordinated or attractive or acceptable they were; rather, their exuberant dance was the overflow of their joy and freedom. And I, as their parent, delighted in their delight. In that moment, in my living room, still puffing from the dance, I chose to believe that's how my Father sees me. In that moment, standing with bare feet in the dusty sunbeams, something was transformed in me. I suddenly saw every way that I stay small to carefully guard myself from rejection. I felt the God who made me invite me to lift my head, to take up space, to be unafraid of the ways my true self might collide with all the things I desperately tried not to be. I had assumed I knew what God meant by "Dance for the healing to come." It had more layers than I'd known! Could it be that the invitation to do hard and strange things is also an invitation toward our own healing? The obedience to things we'd never choose releases us from trying desperately to be the people we think we are and to have the things we think we need. These restraints have been digging into our skin for so long that at first, release is painful. But it's a kind of pain that leads to freedom.

I had long since stopped trying to figure out if I was flying like a goose or rediscovering my childlike instincts or listening to the Spirit. Whatever this was had little regard for cultural stereotypes. The healing I was discovering made me trust what was working itself out in me. But in some ways that made it harder because I couldn't always explain what was going on to those who wanted explanations. Part of me recognized in them the same hesitations I had. If I was trying hard not to let my self-talk bully my instincts, I didn't need someone else's words demanding the same rationalizations I was trying not to demand of myself. How could I explain to someone else why I was doing what I was doing when I couldn't explain it to myself? I didn't have enough understanding to reassure myself, much less anyone else. And I knew that just saying "God told me" could easily become another kind of power abuse. I was in this strange netherworld, being disrupted by these inner prompts and yet not being able to set them aside. Not only was it making me uncomfortable but it was also making some key people in my

FIELD GUIDE

What stereotypes are you trying to avoid? Are there caricatures related to your body type, socioeconomic status, family background, gender, race, age, or personality that cause you to feel shame? How did you learn to be ashamed of those parts of yourself? How do you live to avoid caricatures?

life uncomfortable. So now I found myself in conflict with the very people whose understanding and support I most needed.

I hate conflict. So why would I continue on this path? And yet when I considered ignoring these new ways of receiving, all of which felt like connection to God, I couldn't imagine how to do that. I wondered if I was losing touch with reality—was this what a Messiah complex feels like? Was I on some kind of a crusade? I know that discerning the Spirit involves asking the community to discern with us. But what about when your community gives you mixed messages? Do you choose to believe the ones who most affirm what you sense in your own spirit? Or do you set aside what seems to be the call of God within you just to keep the peace?

My journal from this time was rather intense, filled with a deep, internal conflict. On the one hand, I was feeling drawn toward something beautiful that I didn't fully understand, and on the other hand, I was feeling the pain when it didn't go as I hoped or when others didn't understand. Here is a sampling of some of my thoughts during this period:

When I'm still learning how to discern your direction, Lord, where do I look for clues that I'm hearing and responding well? If others don't like or agree with what I'm doing and saying, when is that a sign that I'm doing it wrong and when is it a sign to press through?

Feeling a little wrung out by the miracle but hopeful that I haven't yet seen the fullness of the miracle.

Often I don't understand the things God calls me to say or do until I watch them take root and blossom in the lives of others.

It would be easier for me not to give words to my hope and longing, not to pray with tears for healing, not to care, not to keep following even when I'm tired and the miracles haven't yet begun.

Verbalizing these thoughts I didn't shape makes me wonder how Mary felt—birthing things she didn't create.

If I'm honest, I often feel my imagination is better than God's. I truly believe he could do anything. So I let myself believe he will do the specific wonderful thing I can imagine. When my hopes are dashed, I stop hoping. I put myself out on a limb (often publicly) but see no immediate fruit so feel God left me hanging (publicly). So I inch back to safety.

I'm learning that I run ahead of God, assuming I know why he's asking me to do something. Then I get resentful and discouraged when it doesn't live up to my expectations.

I long to see you, Lord. Don't let that longing be my undoing.

It takes courage and perseverance to live in the space between leaping and landing.

I have to trust that if the Spirit is prompting me to act/speak/pray/write/long, the same Spirit will equip me to do what I'm prompted to do.

Confessing the vagueness, not just powering through it, seems to help others be open to what I'm saying.

What does it mean to be called to challenge when I long to make peace?

What does it look like to be called to be a voice of difference when I long to belong?

While it was painful to continue to explore these possibilities, I couldn't set them aside. I wanted the impossible combination of the safety of old habits and the joyful possibilities inherent

FIELD GUIDE

Do any of these reflections or questions resonate with you? Which ones? How?

in new, risky habits. At the time it only felt like confusion. I see now that I was driven on by a sense of what could be. I was driven on by a taste of Joy, which C. S. Lewis gives a capital letter, a Christian name. He says, "Joy . . . must have the stab, the pang, the inconsolable longing."[1] A final journal entry sums it up: "It helps me to imagine that this stab, this pang, this inconsolable longing are connected to joy. Why would I keep pursuing unless I felt a joy for where it would lead me? It's easy to focus on the longing for what is lacking and forget the joy of what I'm drawn toward. In my inconsolable longing I have found comfort in the possibility that it's a tiny piece of God's longing. How beautiful to think this pang may be part of God's joy!"

I discovered a new hunger to read all the responses people in Scripture give to God when he asks them to do things they don't understand or want to do. Jeremiah's soon became my favorite. As the story opens in Jeremiah, God declares: "Before you were born . . . I appointed you as a prophet to the nations" (1:5). Quite a lot to ask. So we can understand Jeremiah's hesitation: "I do not know how to speak; I am too young." When we sense the overwhelming call of God, whether it's as a prophet to the nations or to say hello to a new neighbor, we see the chasm between the person we are and the person who can accomplish the task. Whether we say it with our mouths or our actions, our impulse is to decline based on feelings of our own inadequacy. Yet we want God to follow our short-sighted reasoning by entering our small world and responding to our self-absorbed

FIELD GUIDE

How does your sense of inadequacy keep you from saying yes to God? How do you want him to assure you of your competence before obeying him?

insecurities with sentences that begin with "You." "You've got this!" "You're smarter than you think!" "You're gifted!" Eugene Peterson's reading of Jeremiah brings this insight: "We are practiced in pleading inadequacy in order to avoid living at the best that God calls us to. . . . If we look at ourselves and are absolutely honest we are always inadequate. . . . Life, in fact, is too much for us."[2] Knowing this about us, God, just as he did with Jeremiah, responds to our self-consciousness by bombarding us with consciousness of himself:

"*I* send you."

"*I* command you."

"*I* am with you to deliver you."

"*I* have put my words in your mouth."

"*I* appoint you."

It's no small thing to overcome a lifelong habit of looking inside ourselves to decide whether and how to say yes to a huge task.

Repenting of Childlike Passivity

As we repent of our adultish ways and enter into childlikeness, we'll find ourselves less and less afraid of normal human powerlessness. This will allow us to be more able to receive insight from the Lord. As we do, we may begin to discover a different kind of temptation: the temptation to be childish.

As we relinquish our own efforts at power, we become more open to the power of the Spirit. And if Jesus's childlike heart toward the Father led him to scary places, even death, we shouldn't be surprised if our childlikeness also leads us to such places. But what a strange conundrum—childlikeness leads us to very serious things. And so we will be tempted to be not simply childlike but childish. If my adultish self was Amanda, my childish self could be called Mandi (preferably with a heart-shaped dot over the "i"). She was comfortable being the unassuming flower child, the artist everyone likes, the soft-spoken introvert who keeps quiet as a way to avoid conflict or misunderstanding. Passivity seems safe. If you never do anything, you can never do anything wrong. Right?

While childlike faith leads us to follow, childishness will bind us in our inadequacy. Rather than leading to childlike dependence, our childish sense of limitation can lead to shame, despair, and passivity. We see this temptation in every Bible character who says "Who am I?" as a way to avoid God's call: in every way that Esther hesitated, in every way that Moses rested in his lack of eloquence, in every way that Jeremiah used his age as an excuse. Underuse of power can be just as much an abuse of power as overuse. It *feels* Christlike because it doesn't grasp for power. But we've created a caricature of Christ. His childlike reliance led to obedience that expressed itself in surprising authority. He was childlike and adultlike— free to be powerless and free to be powerful, reflecting both "ever-expanding consciousness and ever-increasing agency."[3]

God's first children in Eden were strangely potent. God gave them power to name and steward creation, to join him as cocreators. There's a surprising humility required in using agency, in putting our gifts out there, in contributing our voices. Children know how to do so in a way that assumes they have something to offer. There's no need to be everything, just to be something. No need to be everyone, just someone. When children share their art, their ideas, their energy, it's with a sure knowledge that they are one part of a whole, one voice in a chorus. When we are driven by the shame of what's missing in us, believing that our one small voice cannot have the force of a whole choir, our ordinary agency can turn corrosive. Unused, it gnaws at our insides; overused, it consumes others. Either way does violence, whether to our own souls or to the souls of others. But agency that has emptied of the need to be everything leads to engagement in a way that trusts we have something to contribute, small though it may be.

ADULTLIKE
Unafrid
to be
powerful

CHILDISH
Afraid to be
powerful

Figure 6.1. How are you afraid to be powerful? What part of that is healthy and what part is your false, childish self at work? Is there a way God is inviting you to embrace your agency? What might it look like to say yes to that?

Our humility now can be the kind that is both obedient and active, willing to take up its cross. We are like David, small enough to know our need for something beyond ourselves yet big enough to step into the fray—even if it's with nothing but a sling. And when our small efforts have big effects, Someone Else will get the glory. Jesus embodied the perfect balance between childlikeness and adultlikeness in setting aside his control in order to be obedient to the will of the Father. Satan wants us in a double-bind, afraid of both our powerlessness and our power. But Jesus embodies a different way that allows us to live, unashamed, in partnership with the One who completes us.

127

Cocreating with God

Jesus shows us what it means to be cocreators. "Co" because we are *part* of the process of making all things new. "Creators" because we are part of the process of *making all things new*! This kingdom is a community that transforms—a collaborative, powerful place. For us to join its becoming, we'll have to reach back to our childhood for a restored awareness of both the discomfort of our limitations and the discomfort of our agency. We'll be free to be both powerless and powerful. In short, we'll be human again. Humans participating in the kingdom of God.

As I was first learning to listen to the Spirit and as that Spirit invited me to trust my childlike instincts, I was keenly aware of the ways the world pushed back. In very real conversations and relationships, I felt resistance. Sometimes this resistance was understandable given my lack of nuance in communicating new and awkward things. But sometimes people spoke in ways that shamed me, tempting me to turn back to both my adultish, outcome-driven Amanda ways and my childish, passive Mandi ways. Although I hate conflict, the beauty of what I was learning was too wonderful to set aside, so I pressed into the ways I was called, even through pain. At moments when the pain was most intense, when the conflict was most real, I went to the Lord with open hands. "Am I mishearing you? Why is there so much pushback if this is from you? I love the things I'm learning, but I hate the discord it's bringing. If I'm wrong, I'll change. Show me." I began to use the metaphor of a marshmallow pushing up against a bulldozer. And I was not the bulldozer in this scenario. I felt so small and insignificant and soft, trying to stand against an iron monstrosity. When I told a friend I felt like a marshmallow pushing against a bulldozer, she said, "I understand why you'd feel like that. But you need a better story." I agreed. So I tried to imagine a better story, which is hard when you feel like a marshmallow pushing up against a bulldozer. I prayed to the Lord of all Stories for a better story. A day or two later I got a cryptic text from my friend: "Read chapters 9–11 of Prince Caspian."

Just as God's kindness had released me from my false Amanda self through the story of *The Little Prince*, he now drew on a long-loved story to release me from my false Mandi self. He knew how much I'd found a friend in Lucy Pevensie—the honest and brave young girl in C. S. Lewis's Chronicles of Narnia—ever since, at around her age, I first joined her on adventures following Aslan, a lion that seemed an awful lot like Jesus. In *Prince Caspian*, Lucy and her three siblings are on a journey, and they're rather desperately lost.[4] Just as Peter, the eldest, has decided the best way forward, Lucy spots Aslan and her eyes shine at the sight. Her older sister, Susan, asks, "Where did you think you saw him?" to which Lucy replies, "Don't talk like a grown-up. I didn't think I saw him. I saw him." Lucy explains that Aslan was standing in a place quite the opposite of where they'd just decided to go and that he wanted them to follow him that way. The children then pick apart Lucy's claims because no one else saw him but Lucy. The older children decide to disregard Lucy and to continue on the path they've already chosen. Their decision to follow what makes sense (to them) brings the chapter to an end with "And Lucy came last of the party, crying bitterly."

The way becomes more difficult than expected and leads them right into a volley of arrows, so they have to crawl all the way back over the ground they'd already traveled. In discouragement, the little band finds a safe place and sets up camp for the night. In the middle of the night, Lucy wakes up with the feeling that "the voice she liked best in the world had been calling her name." She assumes it's just a dream, but when she continues to hear the voice she finally gets up to follow it through the trees, which somehow seem to be dancing. As she dances among them, she comes to a circle of grass. "And then—oh joy! For he was there: the huge Lion, shining white in the moonlight." Lucy rushes toward her Aslan, burying her face in his mane. As they speak, Aslan isn't pleased that Lucy tries to blame the others for the delays of the day. She cries, "I couldn't have left the others and come up to you alone, how could I? Don't look at me like that . . . oh well, I suppose I *could*. Yes, and it wouldn't have been alone, I know, not if I was with you. But what would have been the good?" When Aslan remains silent, she continues, "You mean that it would have turned out all right? . . . Am I not to know?"

Aslan responds with a challenge: "To know what would have happened, child? Nobody is ever told that. But anyone can find out what will happen. If you go back to the others now, and wake them up; and tell them you have seen me again; and that you must all get up at once and follow me—what will happen? There is only one way of finding out."

Lucy is understandably afraid. She knows they won't believe her, that it will cause conflict again, and maybe they will shame her again. Finally, in her anguish, Lucy buries her head in his mane, and as she does, she feels his lion-strength entering her. Aslan breathes these words over her: "Now you are a lioness. And now all Narnia will be renewed."

With that, Lucy returns to the challenge of waking her siblings, to tell them, once again, that she has seen Aslan and they must follow him. The argument about whether to trust her begins again and hurtful things are said, but this time something is different. This time Lucy chooses to follow Aslan herself, even if no one else will come. And although no one else can see Aslan, Lucy's determination prompts them—eventually—to follow her lead. One by one, as they walk in the darkness, they begin to see Aslan for themselves.

At that critical juncture, I needed Lucy's story. It gave me grace for all the ways I was like Lucy—making wrong choices, avoiding hard things, misunderstanding my part. Sometimes I'm the Susan to someone else's Lucy. In every way any of us "sees Aslan," it's our job just to follow him, to trust that even if at first others don't see him, something about our following, if we're not reactionary and accusatory, might open up new possibilities. We have to trust that others might come to see how our willingness to take a risk might become something more meaningful to them than our bargaining and defensiveness. When they begin to see what we see, we'll find new ways of learning together, new affirmation of things we worried we were only imagining.

Only now did I see how much I'd been trying to defend my decisions to follow in an empire way of sharing kingdom things. I'd been waiting until friends and colleagues agreed before I actually stepped forward. This was partly because I loved their acceptance and partly because I hated the thought of breaking a connection with them. And, if I'm honest, maybe I also wanted to convince them to go first. But this story of Lucy gave me courage to imagine that if what I was sensing was truly from God then it was right for all of us. And if it wasn't, I would learn that too.

I'd been taught my whole life that consensus was a sign of God's will (and there are certainly times when disagreement means we should reconsider). But now I was discovering that there are also times when we are asked to be the first to speak, and our very action will bring something new. For a people-pleaser and consensus-seeker like me it was powerful to read these words from Anna Carter Florence: "Can I really say that . . . if the authorities say something different? Can I really say that . . . if no one will support me, let alone believe me? Can I really say that . . . if it sounds crazy, even to me? Can I really say that . . . if it puts my word and life at risk? Can I really say that . . . if I am only one person, with no special power? Can I really say that . . . even though I have no proof beyond what I have seen and believed?"[5]

These old, childish, passive instincts were good at putting Christian language around the disobedience of avoiding my own agency. And I'd come to see these instincts in Jeremiah's "But I'm only a child" response and Lucy's avoidance of Aslan's first invitation. While it's not a common word in contemporary discipleship, in Christian history the name for this sin is acedia.

Acedia, then, is a profound withdrawal into self. Action is no longer perceived as a gift of oneself, as the response to a prior love that calls us, enables our action, and makes it possible. It is seen instead as an uninhibited seeking of personal satisfaction in the fear of "losing" something. The desire to save one's "freedom" at any price reveals, in reality, a deeper enslavement to the "self." There is no longer any room for an abandonment of the self to the other or for the joy of gift; what remains is sadness or bitterness within the one who distances himself from the community and who, being separated from others, finds himself likewise separated from God.[6]

And so, just as we have had to set aside all things adultish to step into childlikeness, we have to set aside all things childish to step into adultlikeness. Mandi is accomplished at saying, "Who am I? Someone better equipped should do it." This might seem self-effacing and Christlike, but it can also mask a quiet kind of power abuse—an unwillingness to own the positive power we have and use it in obedience. It can also mask a surprising pride demonstrated by an overinflated trust in our own assessment of ourselves and an underestimation of God's power to change and use us. We all would love to avoid responsibility. Mandi would much rather be skipping in the grass than speaking from a pulpit. But if she's called by God to speak from a pulpit, to avoid it is disobedience.

How can we step into whatever agency is ours without overstepping into God's role? We like resting and receiving. What will we do when resting and receiving call us to respond? How can we live as God's children without a childish avoidance of how he is calling us into action? If he is both delighting in his own creation and engaging in his mission to make it all new, how can both childlike wonder and adultlike agency help us join him and partner with him in new ways?

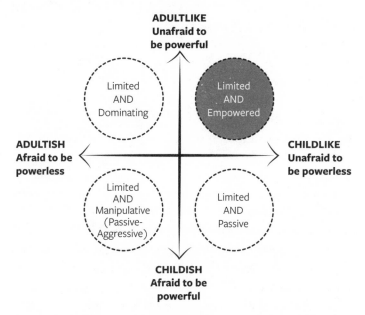

Figure 6.2. While this process of growing toward adultlikeness/childlikeness is not scientific, how does this matrix help you discern your tendencies? What quadrant is your natural habitat? What will it look like to move up and to the right, where Jesus lived?

Mary, the mother of Jesus, embodies this life that sets aside power and agenda in order to live out the terrifying reality of our own agency in the way God wants us to use it. Luke 1 sets up a curious comparison between Zechariah and Mary, and while Zechariah is not exactly the bad guy, Mary is the one to watch. Zechariah is older and a man, a leader of the religious establishment, someone with influence. Mary, on the other hand, is young and a woman and nobody special. Zechariah has longed for a child with his wife, Elizabeth, while Mary is not yet married—a situation where sudden news of a pregnancy is not typically welcome. And yet, when they each have an angel appear to them, they have very different reactions.

Zechariah's initial reaction is not a response to the miraculous part of the announcement, the fulfillment of all that Israel has been awaiting. Instead, he responds to the practical matters, and his question is one of doubt: "How can I know this for certain? My wife and I are old." As a result, the angel strikes him dumb, unable to tell the story until the day his son is born. Only then, months after the announcement of this blessing, Zechariah finally has words of praise for God. He's not a terrible guy and we understand his doubts. It's just good to pay attention to how his adultish habits—his value for control, power, and understanding—almost made him miss the miracle.

Mary has a different story. When the angel visits her to tell her this strange news, even though it's both more scandalous and more miraculous than Zechariah's news, her response is one of willingness. She responds not only to the practical matters but also to the eternal promises that are being fulfilled. She responds with acceptance of this thing that is already at work within her own body, and she is able to rejoice before she even sees the child. Her song is remembered as one of Scripture's most profound expressions of praise. Mary is not perfect, but she has practiced these postures of resting and receiving, partly because, as a person on the margins, she has had no other choice. Perhaps this is why she is chosen for this role of raising the Son of God. She knows what it is to set aside striving and receive as a child. Her childlikeness allows her to accept the role she has been given. At the same time, she knows what it is to set aside passivity and respond as an adult. She knows what it means to partner with God, at work in this world. And because of her faithfulness, she allows God to reveal himself, through her simple life, to all humanity. "Mary can't be ranked between passivity and activity because she breaks the mold."[7] She had to be like a child to receive the kingdom. She had to be like an adult to bear the kingdom.

It's easy to romanticize the role of Mary in the story of Jesus, to wish we could have been so close to the miracle. And yet we can't fully comprehend the kind of whole-body obedience that was required of her, to submit her will and her life so that the kingdom could be birthed through her. We remember that she was blessed by angels, held the infant Jesus, and got to see prophecies fulfilled on a daily basis. But her kind of obedience also meant joining Jesus in his suffering—a sword would pierce her own soul too. We shouldn't be surprised if, as it did for Mary, this childlikeness that allows us to welcome the kingdom also takes us into very serious, adult situations. And if Jesus was the ultimate example of a faithful child of the Father, we shouldn't be surprised if, as it did for him, our childlike following takes us to suffering.

When Obedience Feels Like Death

I took a second retreat to Gethsemani Abbey several years after my first. I had by now gotten into the habit of childlike wonder and reveled in the opportunity to take my sweet time. However, on this visit there was a deep pain undergirding all

> "A way of envisaging this experience of opening ourselves to the Christ child is to use the example of Mary pregnant with Jesus. She creates a space for the Christ child to dwell and indeed to develop. In the sense that the word can be born in each person, Mary is the mother of us all and an example to us all."
>
> Fiona Gardner, *The Only Mind Worth Having:*
> *Thomas Merton and the Child Mind*

the wonder. Learning to trust those childlike instincts had not only opened my eyes to delight but also awakened other instincts that led me into places I wouldn't have chosen to go—to pray for things I wasn't yet seeing, to proclaim things I had a hard time imagining, to work as if things were possible when they felt impossible, to say yes to God even if it meant conflict with others. I was tired and discouraged. God felt far away. Maybe I'd misheard him; maybe I'd responded in the wrong way; maybe I was expecting too much. Maybe he'd forsaken me.

In the library at Gethsemani I came across a rather grotesque bust of suffering Jesus. My first response was annoyance. The art snob in me dismissed it as bad art—wounded puppy-dog eyes wanting my pity when I'm just trying to find a book to read. And suddenly everywhere I went Jesus was suffering. He looked down at me from the cross in the dining room, ruining my morning tea and toast. (Jeez, Jesus. I'm trying to relax here.) In my tradition we have plenty of crosses, but they're usually bare. We want to focus on the resurrected Lord. In this very Catholic setting it didn't surprise me to find Jesus still suffering everywhere I went, but it did bum me out. Until I went for spiritual direction with Father Carlos, who wisely presented me with a new perspective. After I swamped this man of silence with a deluge of tearful words, he simply asked, "What do you do with your suffering?" I squinted back, "Is there an option? I try to avoid it of course!" What else could I do? And to one life-altering question he added another: "What if the suffering isn't yours?"

FIELD GUIDE

How do you usually respond to images of a suffering Jesus?

Thankfully I can say my life has not been entirely defined by suffering. I have not experienced some of the deepest terrors that life can dish out. But I've had enough pain to know how pain feels. I've felt the gnawing ache left where something or someone used to be. I've known the devastation of shattered bonds. I've had my fair share of broken dreams. Above all of these, the most significant source of pain has been the pain of feeling abandoned by God. Some emotional pain is like a flesh wound—it's real but it can be localized. With that kind of pain, the unharmed remainder of you can view the pain with some distance, knowing most of you is okay. But the pain of feeling abandoned by God took over my whole body. Every cell was steeped in it, no part of me was untouched. Where do you find hope in forsakenness if it is the source of your hope that seems to have forsaken you? It had both the familiar ache of loss and the devastation of broken relationship. The empty space where I used to feel God's closeness was itself the source of the pain.

It was some time before I understood the twist in the story that contorted my heart. Not only did I feel forsaken by God, it was my obedience to God that had brought me here. I had only done these things that left me feeling alone because he'd prompted me to. I had only gone to these places that terrified me because he'd led me there. And the place where these prompts led me looked nothing like the rosy glow of his prompt. Instead of a garden, I found myself in a desert.

I'd been in seasons when following God felt like life and growth. This desert was the opposite of whatever that was. It meant waking up every day and setting aside what I'd like to do and choosing instead to do what he asks. It meant pushing through the sadness of what I'm missing out on to do this. It sometimes meant overriding my normal, human self-preservation instinct to step into places that felt unsafe, to make choices that made me look foolish, to dare to care about broken things that might never be fixed.

I believe our way of life should lead to joy. I was still taking time to pay attention to the way of the clouds, the sound of the birds, but it didn't always pay off in the form of delight in the way it once had. I didn't often feel God's pleasure.

God does not test us with more than we can bear.

At the same time, he disciplines those he loves.

God leads us into life and growth.

At the same time, he prunes us.

We have space in our minds for martyrs—people who die in obvious, sudden ways because of their faith. We know their stories from the Bible and church history. We understand this is part of the Christian story. But what about the kind of martyrdom that slowly draws the life from us, not in an execution but from a daily life of being poured out like a drink offering?

In a career-oriented culture, where we easily equate our Christian mission with fulfillment and life goals, what will we do with these scriptural descriptions of our call?

> If any want to become my followers, let them deny them-
> selves and take up their cross daily and follow me.
> (Luke 9:23 NRSV)

> For those who want to save their life will lose it, and those
> who lose their life for my sake, and for the sake of the
> gospel, will save it. (Mark 8:35 NRSV)

In a culture that loves to measure success, what are we to think about the example of the prophets? Their story is one of being called to say and do ridiculous things to an unhearing, uncaring people. It's a story of hammering on hard hearts. Prophets were dared by God to feel his own pain, to long for things they would never see. Will we risk equating our story with the martyrs and the prophets, as ordinary as we are? (Whenever I do, I hear the self-accusation, "Who are you to compare yourself to Jeremiah?!") It may be the only way our own story can make sense. Those stories of martyrs and prophets may help us to set aside other stories we're tempted to believe. Twisted stories like this:

> If you're not seeing fruit, it's because you're doing it wrong.
> If your work never feels finished, just work harder.
> When prayers aren't answered, it's because you're unfaithful.
> When solutions don't come, it's because God is not with you.
> When you feel like you're not getting anywhere, it's because you're just not very good at this.
> When things seem to fall into place for other Christians, when their efforts seem more successful, their families more happy, it's a sign that you're out of God's favor.
> When you don't see God making all things new, it's because God has forsaken you. Or forgotten his promises. Or maybe he doesn't even exist.

Obedience to the kind of life we're called to will not always feel good. This flies in the face of our cultural expectations of success. Of course, this kind of discomfort may mean it's time to discern if we're in the right place. It may be a sign that we need to grow or something needs to change. But when we've discerned those things and still following God is hard, when we've prayed for a release from the discomfort and no change comes, when we're doing our best to care for ourselves and this obedience still takes more than it gives, it may simply be that this is the life that obedience has led us to.

In one of his last concerts, Rich Mullins said this:

> When I read the lives of most of the great saints they didn't necessarily feel very close to God. When I read the Psalms I get the feeling like David and the other Psalmists felt quite far away

from God for most of the time. Closeness to God is not about feelings, closeness to God is about obedience. . . . I don't know how you feel close to God. And no one I know that seems to be close to God knows anything about those feelings either. I know if we obey occasionally the feeling follows, not always, but occasionally. I know that if we disobey we don't have a shot at it.[8]

This life of obedience will likely call us to say yes to things we don't want to say yes to.

We may be called to say goodbye to people we would rather be with, to be with people we would not choose. We may be called to stay in places we would rather leave, leave places when we would rather stay. He may call us to say things that make us feel stupid, to do things that feel dangerous. He may call us to long for healing for someone who may never be healed, to care for someone who may never be "fixed."

All this may feel like death. Overriding our self-preservation instincts, pressing against our own wills, and giving up our time and energy and control all feel like death in slow doses. We may not give these deaths as much weight as physical death, but what is a life if not our will and time and energy? Jesus died many deaths before he died on the cross. This is living sacrifice. Living sacrifice will sometimes make us feel far from God. If we understand his presence only as comfort and ease, then it's hard to feel his presence in suffering. If we've become accustomed only to the joy of childlikeness, we may not grow

---

FIELD GUIDE

How has obedience felt like death for you? How has following God led to difficulty or confusion? How can obedience—even when it doesn't lead to expected outcomes—become an opportunity for closeness with God?

in our capacity for adultlikeness. As we own our agency, there's a strange kind of closeness to God hidden even in this rather daunting kind of obedience.

Feels Like Death, Looks Like Life

According to Paul we carry around in our bodies the death of Jesus, so that his very life may be visible in our bodies (2 Cor. 4:10). While we are constantly living lives that daily become less and less our own, Jesus's own life becomes more and more evident. Not just in a measurable outcome we produced but in our actual bodily witness. This body, buried slowly, over the course of a whole life—a very slow kind of martyrdom—might bear witness to a different way of life. After all, the Greek word for "witness" is the root of the English word "martyr." To present our bodies as a living sacrifice every day is to, in our bodies, bear witness to the story of Jesus. As we become less and Jesus becomes more, what feels to us like death may look to others very much like life.[9]

While this may not bring the kind of flourishing our younger selves imagined when we first began responding to God's prompts, this life of obedience certainly brings a strange kind of flourishing. As, day by day, we slowly die to our own preferences and desires, it may feel like being buried. But with Christ's example we come to see that burial as a planting of something hopeful in the soil—something that dies only to burst into life. So we come to live out Jesus's promise and his own story: "Very truly I tell you, unless a kernel of wheat falls to the ground and dies, it remains only a single seed. But if it dies, it produces many seeds" (John 12:24).

As I began to embrace this I journaled the following:

> When I chose to be a farmhand
> It was because I'd tasted the fruit.

I wanted to make more, enough for everyone.
I had visions of fields, crammed with plants, laden with
   fruit.

I had no idea I'd be farming the desert.

I want to believe this ground is fertile.
I want to believe these seeds are good.
I have to ask, "Am I doing it wrong?"

I ask the Farmer every morning
And as I do, he fills my hands with tiny, bright seeds.
His eyes shine with what he knows they'll be
And to my questions he just smiles and says, "Sow."

This call that seems beyond us, these prayers we're called to pray that threaten to break our hearts, these things we're asked to give that we fear will leave us with nothing: How could God ask so much of us? Doesn't he know we're only clay vessels? Doesn't he realize that pouring his love and longing into our small, brittle hearts might break us? Can't he see the way of following him is too much for us? And yet all my resentful questions led to God posing a strange question of his own.

I had gushed to a friend about all the ways it was too much. She said it sounded like I was trying to catch the ocean in a tiny cup. With indignation toward God I exclaimed, "Yes, that's exactly what it feels like!" I imagined this brittle clay vessel being asked to contain mighty, turbulent waters. It doesn't take much to imagine the fate of a fragile cup at the mercy of ocean waves. I waited for God to draw back the seas to let this cup pass. Something had to change, and I assumed it would be him. That would have made logical sense. This was too much for me, and God does not ask for more than anyone can handle; therefore, he had to change his expectations. Instead he asked, "What if the clay is still wet?"

I remembered again my old friend Jeremiah. When he followed the prompts of the Spirit they took him to much darker places than these prompts have (yet) taken me. Jeremiah's obedience to God meant speaking against his own people, calling Israel back to her God. And they did not thank Jeremiah for this reminder. Instead, Jeremiah's obedience to the prompts of the Spirit meant his own people began to plot against him in order to cut him off from the land of the living so that his name would be forgotten (Jer. 11:19). Jeremiah feels like a foolish, gentle lamb, being led off to slaughter. He cries out to God since he's only in this uncomfortable and dangerous situation because God led him here. We, along with Jeremiah, hope that God will say, "Oh, I'm so sorry! I had no idea it would cost you so much. You don't have to do what I said." Instead, God tells him, "If you have raced with men on foot and they have worn you out, how can you compete with horses?" (12:5). Which seems cruel. God is basically saying, "You ain't seen nothing yet!" I could imagine Jeremiah was tempted, like me, to see himself as a brittle clay vessel, straining to contain all God has asked of him, begging that this fragile vessel be spared. And instead of changing his plans, God asks Jeremiah to change his imagination: "What if the clay is still wet?"

It's important to come to a place of acknowledging our smallness, of feeling the ordinary clay we are. It's a moment to confront the truth of our own humanness. While empire shames humanness, kingdom loves it. Kingdom knows *humanness* can be a place that welcomes *Godness*. And then kingdom can come. As that clay vessel becomes filled with that unfading treasure of the Spirit, that Spirit brings new life. That Spirit wants to go, to speak, to act, to give, to love, to challenge. This Spirit is a force of life—eternal life—housed in this small body, a partnership possible only if we are willing to set aside all the ways we've been trying to be big enough, full enough. But at some point, once God's presence becomes comfortable in this clay vessel, that Spirit may begin stretching the clay and prompting this body to go places, do things, speak words, proclaim truths that we're sure will break us.

Barbara Brown Taylor makes a vital distinction between pain and suffering.

> There is a difference between pain and suffering, which I have used as synonymous until now. . . . More often than not, you can lay your hands on pain. You can find the place that hurts. . . . Suffering, on the other hand, happens in the mind. The mind decides what pain means and whether it is deserved. . . . The mind remembers how good things used to be and are not likely to be again. The mind makes judgments, measures loss, takes blame, and assigns guilt. . . . According to Job, his pain is like being pierced by poisonous arrows. . . . But . . . Job's suffering surpasses it, as he asks God to explain what has happened to him and receives no answer. . . . Thus Job suffers from God's silence, which hurts him worse than his boils, worse than his poverty, worse even than the death of his children.[10]

We're confronted, like Job, with both pain and suffering. This experience is painful, and obedience to God brought me to this pain. Now, in addition to the pain of my circumstances, there is the suffering of our interpretation of the pain. And God does not ask us to pretend there's no pain but to repent from

FIELD GUIDE

Where are you feeling called to die so that something will grow? Where are you feeling called to remain pliable so that God can expand your capacity?

our assumption that pain is forsakenness. God enters into the crisis not with the desired release from the painful circumstance but with an interpretation that alleviates the suffering. He asks, "Will you let the clay be wet? Will you let your capacity for love, for longing, for justice, for truth, for adventure be stretched? Will you let my fullness be revealed in and through you, because of and in spite of you?" If we do, we may find ourselves learning the very heart of God.

> If the LORD had not been on our side . . .
>> the flood would have engulfed us,
> the torrent would have swept over us,
>> the raging waters
> would have swept us away. (Ps. 124:1, 4–5)

For the Joy Set before Him

I wonder how far ahead Jesus knew his own story. We see along the way that he has glimpses of what's about to unfold. But what if, like us, he just rested in the Father each day and received from the Father each day and responded to what he received? And each day, the prompts took him deeper into the Father's will . . . and deeper into danger. Something drives him on, some vision of Reality is under his skin and nothing can deter him from it. It costs him, too, even before he gets to Golgotha. Throughout Mark 14 and 15 we watch as the stakes get higher,

"He is no fool who gives what he cannot keep to gain that which he cannot lose."

Jim Elliot, quoted by Elisabeth Elliot, *The Shadow of the Almighty: The Life and Testament of Jim Elliot* and Jesus just keeps following where childlikeness takes him. In five scenes Mark shows us various opportunities Jesus had to step toward empire but, at every turn, he chooses kingdom.

First, Mark invites us to a meal where a woman upsets the proceedings by pouring a jar of perfume worth a year's salary on Jesus's head. She goes against all sense of decorum and common sense. What a scene! What a waste! Her behavior flies in the face of all that empire values. But she is anointing a different kind of king. And unlike the others in the room, Jesus welcomes her actions. He embraces this outcast who knows the abandon and the abundance of kingdom. The others misunderstand, they shame, they disregard. He could choose to acquiesce to their expectations of him. But Jesus is driven by something better than their approval. In pressing toward it, he dies this social death.

Next, we're welcomed into another room and another meal. This time Jesus celebrates Passover with his disciples and, even as they eat, Jesus predicts that one of them will betray him and that the rest will desert and deny him. At the moment when their friend needs them the most, when he is most clear about who he is and what the kingdom requires of him, they will flee. Knowing this will happen, Jesus could just drop the plan, go back to a normal life, set aside the conflict that his choices are bringing. But he presses on toward kingdom, even when he knows his own friends will choose comfort and safety (and, in some cases, empire). In pressing toward kingdom, Jesus dies this relational death.

Then Mark takes us to the scene in the garden of Gethsemane and lets us see just how much Jesus is breaking under the weight of this kingdom vision. The waves threaten to smash this clay vessel to pieces. He throws himself to the ground in distress, agitated beyond description. He cries out to the Father as a child cries, torn between a desire to be obedient and a deep, bodily sense of what it will cost. Will this emptying of his will leave him with no self left? And even in the face of his friends' rejection, even in the midst of this angst, Jesus again chooses kingdom. In so doing, Jesus dies an emotional and existential death. It's important to see, with Thomas Keating, the extent of his sacrifice: "Christ's sacrifice of himself for us . . . is not only his death on the cross, but the psychological, spiritual and personal alienation. . . . When our sufferings are joined to Christ's they become redemptive for us personally."[11]

The day should be dawning after this excruciating night, but Mark's telling only gets darker as we find Jesus facing a trial before the religious leaders. Empire is looking for a reason to put him to death. Empire asks "Are you?" and Jesus says "I am." It's all empire needs to hear to do away with him. He could have continued his silence. He could have questioned his own call. He could have returned to Nazareth. But once more something better than safety drew him forward. He has already died to social status, emotional security and existential equilibrium, and his own will. Now, in the face of impending physical harm, he dies to his own self-preservation instinct. He dies to any claim empire might have on him. He does so because of the claim that kingdom has on him. These deaths allow him to welcome the kingdom as a child. And then comes the final death.

Mark describes a strange, midday darkness that comes over the whole land, casting a shadow over the Son of God, dying on a cross. With his final breath, Jesus cries, "My God, My God, why have you forsaken me?" (Mark 15:34). Is this a cruel trick that the joy of seeking the kingdom led him toward what feels like hell? The longing for connection with the Father has brought Jesus to the suffering of separation from him.

Yet I have to wonder: Did the Father *actually* forsake Jesus? Or was Jesus following the ancient pattern of lament that we see in the Psalms? What if he had childlike freedom to express his *feeling* of being abandoned? Maybe this was not Jesus seizing one final opportunity to make a theological statement but a deeply human release of emotion. As we have seen, there's a difference between the very real feeling of being forsaken and actual forsakenness. In Job's story, in addition to the pain of the circumstances, there's the added suffering of wondering where God is and why he's allowing this. In addition to the excruciating physical pain Jesus experiences, there's the very real emotional and spiritual torment—I'm only here because I said yes to every prompt of the Spirit. I'm only here because I chose to be a child, welcoming the kingdom. Why would a good God reward me in this way for my obedience? It's how we all feel when obedience feels like death. There's a long and rich Jewish tradition of crying out when we feel that way.[12]

I have to wonder if Mark's intent is not only to record this single exclamation of Jesus but also to draw attention to the entire psalm Jesus references. Although Psalm 22 was written centuries before Jesus's birth, the words seem tailored for his use on the cross:

> My God, my God, why have you forsaken me?
>> Why are you so far from saving me,
>> so far from my cries of anguish? . . .
> All who see me mock me;
>> they hurl insults, shaking their heads.
> "He trusts in the LORD," they say,
>> "let the LORD rescue him.
> Let him deliver him,
>> since he delights in him." . . .
> Roaring lions that tear their prey
>> open their mouths wide against me.
> I am poured out like water,
>> and all my bones are out of joint.
> My heart has turned to wax;
>> it has melted within me.
> My mouth is dried up like a potsherd,
>> and my tongue sticks to the roof of my mouth;
>> you lay me in the dust of death.

Dogs surround me,
　　a pack of villains encircles me;
　　they pierce my hands and my feet.
All my bones are on display;
　　people stare and gloat over me.
They divide my clothes among them
　　and cast lots for my garment. (vv. 1, 7–8, 13–18)

In empire, when we experience suffering, we try to understand it, we try to overcome it and escape it. We do all in our power to alleviate our misery, and if we finally decide God has forsaken us, we forsake him. But a child who suffers responds like one without power. A child cries out for help to a power greater than his own. A child knows there is a place to wail, to proclaim in great detail the state of his soul, his mind, his body. And once the sobbing is over, there is release and the calm of new possibilities, as we see in many psalms of lament, including Psalm 22, which weaves back and forth from words of anguish to words of praise:

Yet you are enthroned as the Holy One;
　　you are the one Israel praises.
In you our ancestors put their trust;
　　they trusted and you delivered them.
To you they cried out and were saved;
　　in you they trusted and were not put to shame. . . .
Yet you brought me out of the womb;
　　you made me trust in you, even at my mother's breast.
From birth I was cast on you;
　　from my mother's womb you have been my God. . . .
You who fear the LORD, praise him!
　　All you descendants of Jacob, honor him!
　　Revere him, all you descendants of Israel!
For he has not despised or scorned
　　the suffering of the afflicted one;

he has not hidden his face from him
    but has listened to his cry for help.
From you comes the theme of my praise in the great
       assembly;
    before those who fear you I will fulfill my vows.
The poor will eat and be satisfied;
    those who seek the Lord will praise him—
    may your hearts live forever!
All the ends of the earth
    will remember and turn to the LORD,
and all the families of the nations
    will bow down before him,
for dominion belongs to the LORD
    and he rules over the nations.
All the rich of the earth will feast and worship;
    all who go down to the dust will kneel before him—
    those who cannot keep themselves alive.
Posterity will serve him;
    future generations will be told about the LORD.
They will proclaim his righteousness,
    declaring to a people yet unborn:
He has done it! (vv. 3–5, 9–10, 23–31)

Perhaps Jesus's potsherd mouth was too parched for a complete recitation. But what a possibility to imagine that those who heard him also knew the psalm he referenced. After all, the onlookers seem to respond to more than the first phrases of the psalm—they offer him a drink (perhaps in response to the psalm's words "my tongue sticks to the roof of my mouth") and wait to see if Elijah will save him (perhaps in response to the entire tone of Psalm 22). And it's possible that Jesus's last words recorded in John's telling, "It is finished!" echo the psalm's last words, "He has done it!"[13]

And if we needed any further proof that the Father had not forsaken him, we only had to wait until Sunday. The Spirit who had prompted him every day of his life, who had led him toward many deaths, also held the pain in every kind of death he died. Even if out of childlike obedience to the Spirit, we, like Jesus, are led to die social and emotional and relational and political and economic and existential and physical deaths, not one of those deaths is beyond the resurrection power of the Spirit. And as we die to every temptation toward empire, kingdom is allowed to grow in us. God did not forsake Jesus in his pain, and God does not forsake us in ours. In fact, it's possible that in pain we come to know him better than ever before.

FIELD GUIDE

To highlight the two voices in Psalm 22—one of despair and one of faithful hope—I've split the psalm to quote them separately. Read Psalm 22 as a whole and take note of how it moves back and forth between these two postures (watch especially for the words "yet" and "but"), giving space for lament and hope all in one psalm. What psalm would you write, using "yet" and "but," expressing every raw emotion, even if they seem in conflict?

CHAPTER 7

A Theology of
Childlikeness

All this lived theology made me revisit the theology I'd read. We've tried to create a system of theology that answers all the questions, to create a ministry model that fixes all the problems. We've worked to say the right prayers to avoid every mess. We've done our best to follow all the rules so God is placated enough to bless us with easy lives. None of it has brought the promises we see in Scripture. We're exhausted, dry, and doubting. And we're wondering where the power of Jesus's gospel went. This gospel that once brought multitudes to him makes little sense even to those of us who've claimed it. Many are walking away from this flat, old Jesus tradition. But maybe there are other options. Maybe the gospel feels powerless because we've tamed it. What if the wild, free, good news of Jesus's life, death, and resurrection actually speaks directly to real pains, hungers, and anxieties we feel every moment? What if his salvation actually saves?

One of the ways that Western culture and Christian faith collide has to do with its experiential nature. Our knowledge about Jesus is fundamentally embodied and subjective. Western theology's discomfort with lived human experience and the resulting efforts to keep faith objective disrupt the very integrity of Christian faith. After years of studying Western theology, nothing had prepared me for the deeply personal, painful, and potentially transformative moments that were nonetheless rich with God's presence. First I questioned my own experience: Was I crazy? Was I a heretic? But with great relief I discovered that there are faithful Christian traditions outside of Western theology that know how to engage both with Scripture and with human experience. So I'm going to tell this story of theological renewal as I experienced it—both in personal, subjective places and in books on theology and history. My lived experience drove me to investigate concepts. Things in books took on life, and things in life found meaning.

Is the Gospel Really Good News?

Let's begin with these questions: How do humans feel lost, and how is the gospel truly good news to that lostness? In the theology we've inherited we often describe a need for salvation through an awareness that we have missed a moral ideal. The sense of need comes from our own guilt—we have done wrong, we have displeased God, fallen short of the glory of God. We feel a void between ourselves and God, a space created as we follow our appetites and run from God's rules. So we've described a cross-shaped bridge that allows humans access to God again (see figure 7.1).

Our traditional presentation of the cross as a bridge has a scriptural background, but it assumes an acknowledgment of God and of his ideals. According to this presentation of our need for God, belief in God is already assumed! Tim Keller

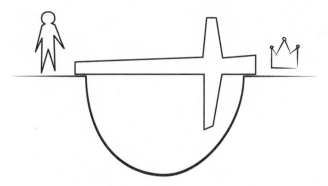

Figure 7.1. The Familiar Cross-Shaped Bridge

describes the paradox: "Past evangelistic strategies assumed that nearly everyone held this shared set of beliefs about a sacred order—that there was a God, an afterlife, a standard of moral truth, and a sense of sin. . . . Today's culture believes the thing we need salvation from is the idea that we need salvation. How, then, do you evangelize people who lack any sense of sin or transcendence, or who lack the traditional basic religious infrastructure such as belief in a Supreme Being or the afterlife?"[1] This cross-shaped bridge is only good news to someone who already feels the void in their ability to live up to God's moral standards.

What a strange, ridiculous problem this leaves us with: we're surprised that we can't explain our worldview to folks who don't already have it, that people who don't know God don't know God! In a culture where those moral standards are no longer assumed and that kind of moral void is rarely felt, our old ways of describing our need for the gospel are becoming less and less meaningful.[2] Maybe the problem is that we ourselves haven't experienced the gospel as good news. The gospel as we've been taught it doesn't connect with actual needs we feel. We haven't experienced Jesus as an answer to our deepest longings. So how can we tell others how it connects to their

FIELD GUIDE

How do you feel your need for salvation? What imagery has been used to help you feel or understand that need? Can you tell stories of how God saved you? If so, what are they? If not, would a new metaphor help?

felt needs, that they're already longing for what Jesus actually offers?

For Western Christians, it seems risky to begin with human experience and trust that the gospel meets us there. But there are places outside of Western Christianity that trust that God designed this salvation specifically for complicated humans like us. "Eastern Orthodox and Celtic Christians have . . . never held a theology of the essential sinfulness of humans as part of their beliefs. Other Christian traditions, however, consider belief in the depravity of humans to be a cornerstone of orthodoxy. Unfortunately, this has led many to mistrust their bodies, emotions, sexuality, intuitions, and much more. This basic mistrust then easily spills over onto others—even onto the natural world. In short, it leaves people cut off from their deepest selves and misaligned with the flow of life."[3] Maybe instead of beginning with bad news—"You know how you're a terrible sinner?"—we can begin with the bad news humans already experience in the dehumanizing system of Western culture and bring good news to that?

Guilt Culture, Shame Culture

Here's an opportunity to investigate how Western culture has shaped this vital theology of the gospel and our need for salvation. Anthropologists and missiologists have known for some time that all cultures fall into three main cultural categories:

Western (guilt) culture, Eastern (shame) culture, and animistic (fear) culture.[4] For any one person, especially one who hasn't had much exposure to other cultures, our own cultural lenses and assumptions are transparent. So let's describe some fundamental assumptions of Western culture and how they affect our theology and reading of Scripture. For our purposes, since we rarely encounter animistic cultures, we'll just compare Western and Eastern cultures.

In the Western way of seeing, the primary concern is our guilt ("I did something wrong") and the primary goal is innocence. This is an individualistic approach that engages primarily through institutions and uses legal metaphors: God is judge. Naturally then, the cross-shaped bridge (penal substitutionary atonement) has been the primary way we've felt the need for, learned, and taught the gospel.

On the other hand, in Eastern culture the primary concern is not guilt but shame. "Shame is a focus on self, guilt is a focus on behavior. Shame is 'I am bad.' Guilt is 'I did something bad.'"[5] Shame has a communal element; it indicates a break in community acceptance that results from our inadequacy or dishonor (e.g., nakedness is not shameful until one is among others). As a result, important Christian images in shame culture are based on family metaphors—God as parent, church as family,

"[Shame] is not just a consequence of something our first parents did in the Garden of Eden. It is the emotional weapon that evil uses to corrupt our relationships with God and each other, and disintegrate any and all gifts of vocational vision and creativity. . . . Shame is a primary means to prevent us from using the gifts we have been given."

Curt Thompson, *The Soul of Shame*

Jesus as sibling. However, Christian theology that engages this culture is largely undeveloped since Eastern cultures are minimally Christian.[6]

While insight into shame culture is significant for Christian workers in places where Eastern culture is prominent, it also has extensive ramifications for the church in Western culture because our own culture is in a state of rapid change. Studies are finding that Western culture is becoming more shame-based because our culture is becoming more and more multicultural, postmodern, and communal.[7] Research also shows that shame culture is particularly predominant for young adults in the West (Gen Z and millennials) as well as highly communal subcultures, as well as for Western women and minorities across generations.[8] For example, Richard Nisbett writes that "[It] is the white Protestants among the American participants in our studies who show the most 'Western' patterns of behavior . . . [while] Catholics and minority group members, including African Americans and Hispanics, are shifted somewhat toward Eastern patterns."[9] While those who shape mainstream culture have been embracing Western, institutional ways for a long time in the Western world (and many minorities have learned these ways as their second language), people living in and shaping alternative cultures have been functioning under the radar in more communal, relational ways. Even in our majority guilt culture many feel a need for God based on shame. And so it's pressing, even within Western culture, that we find ways to understand and communicate the gospel's teaching about shame.[10] We need to rediscover how much this Scripture of ours relates directly to that shame (and always has).

Ironically, the very Scripture on which Western Christianity is built was written by and for not Western but Eastern thinkers. And the Bible relates more naturally to Eastern culture than to Western culture. However, our Western interpretations of this Eastern Scripture make it irrelevant to those from an Eastern culture. In other words, the ways we've read the Bible to apply it to our culture for the past five hundred years will not be meaningful for what our culture is currently becoming. Many are walking away from the Bible because our five-hundred-year-old (mis)interpretations mean nothing to them—the good news seems irrelevant. It's time for us to learn to read the Bible afresh.

E. P. Sanders's insights into Palestinian Judaism breathe freshness into our way of reading the New Testament, especially in our understanding of passages about law and salvation. In our Western perspective we think of law as an impersonal institution and guilt as an individual infraction of those laws, and we bring that understanding into our reading of the New Testament. But Sanders writes that salvation is concerned with being "'in' rather than 'out.'"[11] If God has created a relational covenant with his people (plural), then to be saved is to behave within that covenant, to remain in relationship with him and his people. We may be guilty of choosing behaviors, and we may regret those choices, but the thing that feels most broken is not a rule but a relationship. We feel the shame of being separated from community/belonging and we long for salvation from that exclusion. N. T. Wright describes Sanders's perspective:

> Judaism in Paul's day was not, as has regularly been supposed, a religion of legalistic works-righteousness. . . . Most Protestant exegetes had read Paul and Judaism as if Judaism was a form of the old heresy . . . according to which humans must pull themselves up by their moral bootstraps and thereby earn justification, righteousness and salvation. No, said Sanders. Keeping the law within Judaism always functioned within a covenantal scheme. God took the initiative. . . . God's grace thus precedes everything that people . . . do in response. The Jew keeps the law out of gratitude, as the proper response to grace—not, in other words, in order to *get* into the covenant people, but to *stay* in. Being "in" in the first place was God's gift.[12]

Table 7.1. Guilt Culture versus Shame Culture

	Guilt Culture	**Shame Culture**
Society	Individualistic	Collectivistic
Existential Question	How can my sins be forgiven so I can be assured of heaven?	How can I be a part of the community to be respected?
Christian Theology	Augustinian, Reformed	Undeveloped
Principal Metaphor	Courtroom (legal)	Community (relational)
Christian Status	Historically Christian	Minimally Christian
The Intention of God	God loves us and has a wonderful plan for our lives.	God created us as children with his honor and glory.
The Human Problem	Our personal sin creates a barrier between us and God (or God's plan for our lives).	Our disloyalty dishonors God, so we are shamefully orphaned.
The Solution of Jesus	As a perfect sacrifice for our sins, Jesus bore the wrath of God's punishment.	As our mediator, Jesus bore our shame, rose to glory, and restored glory to God's name.
Salvific Response	Accept Jesus as our personal Savior and pray for forgiveness, turn from human morality	Give allegiance to God, receive adoption into his family, turn from false status

Adapted from Jayson Georges, *The 3D Gospel: Ministry in Guilt, Shame, and Fear Cultures* (n.p.: Timē Press, 2017).

If I'm honest, I've never felt compelled by the cross-shaped bridge. The most guilt I've felt is due to the lack of guilt that seems to be a requirement for Christian faith. I do, however, feel a deep, aching emptiness, a seed of smallness[13] that tells me something's wrong with me. This shame tells me not that I've *done* something wrong (which I might hope to change) but that I *am*, by my very nature, wrong, unwelcome, unacceptable, outside.

This insight into shame culture is how I've come to experience—for the first time—the gospel as truly transformative good news. It's good news that actually responds to needs I feel on a daily basis and brings life and healing to those painful, broken, shameful places. When, at eleven years old, I chose to make this faith my own, it wasn't based on guilt or feeling a need for forgiveness but on a decision to receive God's love for me in a deeper way. Of course, I continue to sin, but rarely in the ways we usually talk about sin—as an abuse of appetites. My sin is harder to pinpoint and often looks like trying to *be* God, which is much worse than eating too much pie or watching the wrong kinds of movies. When you're trying to *be* God you feel pretty close to (being) him, so why would you ever need a cross-shaped bridge? I may have had adultish, Western habits of self-sufficient problem-solving, but they were driven by the more Eastern culture of shame. Shame was my motivation to work hard to stay on top of things, to desperately do everything I could to ensure no one ever saw the ways I wasn't enough.

I've most tried to be God when it comes to knowing and controlling my own destiny. I've given my life to God, but, if I'm honest, it has been a mix of true submission and submission as a way to ensure success. If God is the source of all wisdom and goodness, then it follows that doing what he wants surely is also a way to ensure that life goes well. When I was eighteen, my then boyfriend and I decided to leave our homeland of Australia to study in the United States and United Kingdom so we could return to Australia to do ministry. One high school graduation ceremony, one wedding, and two long flights later, we found ourselves living on the other side of the planet. For ten years we traveled and studied, always giving our lives to the God whom we presumed would eventually bring us back home. Then things hit a wall. The place we'd hoped to work—back in our beautiful hometown, close to family— had no jobs to offer us. The only opportunity that opened its doors was in the United States. So we reasoned, "We'll do this for two years until something opens up in Australia. We've given our lives to the God who wants us to live and minister in Australia. Two years is plenty of time for God to remember that's what he wants."

But *I* was the one who wanted to live and minister in Australia. Every week I scoured the internet looking for job postings. And every month or two, we applied for something in Australia. We were continually interviewing, searching, putting life on hold. I'd chosen the school for our kids, and it was ten thousand miles away; all the while, I hardly knew my neighbors. With each job interview my prayers grew to fever pitch—more so with each failed attempt. I just wanted to go home to have the safety net of parents, the safety net of familiar culture, so my kids could grow up with their cousins. I wanted to eat and talk and live like an Australian. And I wanted the same for my kids. Was that too much to ask?

This two-year stay in the United States became an eight-year stay. And then we had the best opportunity we'd ever had to return to Australia. Finally our kids could actually begin their lives, and we could buy a house and some furniture! We started pricing international moving companies, and the grandparents let themselves dream about making a playroom for our kids. But at the last minute, a very short email put an end to all the excitement. It also put an end to something in me. I'd never sensed I had a hope engine before until it ground to a halt. The voice in me that for ten years had been saying "Maybe next time!" could no longer find the words, along with the part of me that prays. I went into a cave that no one else could find, and it took all my energy to emerge occasionally to pretend I was still in this world—because I didn't want to be. I'd thought I knew what God wanted for me. I'd given everything to make that happen. And it hadn't happened. Over and over and over again. Maybe if I'd just phoned that one place to ask about jobs. Or emailed that one person or gone to that website or conference or subscribed to that job list. Maybe I just hadn't prayed the right prayers.

My Western education had taught me to be resourceful, work hard, never give up. But now I had come to the end of myself. Every resource in me was exhausted, and I was still far short of my goal. Beyond the sadness of my situation, the deeper pain was my feeling of failure. I had no power to do the thing I believed God had told us to do. There was an aching void between what I felt God needed me to be (the savior of our family) and what I actually was (an ordinary human with limited abilities). Oddly, I was ashamed that I had fallen short of my ability to be something God had never asked me to be: God himself. Now, not only was I not in Australia, I didn't want to live on this planet at all—at least for a while. I needed good news.

Although I know now that the gospel has something to offer to heal this aching void I'd discovered in myself, I'd never been taught the gospel that way. In no way did I feel I should repent but rather that *God* should. I was the victim of *his* cruel actions. Why had he put me in charge of making his will happen? I felt no need for a cross-shaped bridge caused by *my* sin. He certainly felt far away, but it was because *he'd* forsaken *me*. *He'd* not come through on (my interpretation of) *his* promises. It's only now that I see my sin of assuming control. I needed to repent of my efforts to *be* God. This was a sin that I'd never heard named. In fact, my culture and education, even in the church, had applauded my every effort to be God! It may be time to name those sins Western culture affirms so that we can come to acknowledge our sin and need for God in new ways.

What new images would allow us to respond to the real pain of the void that we feel every day? Let's look again at José Ortega y Gasset's surprisingly hopeful image of shipwreck:

> And this is the simple truth—that to live is to feel oneself lost—he who accepts it has already begun to find himself, to be on firm ground. Instinctively, as do the shipwrecked, he will

look round for something to which to cling, and that tragic, ruthless glance, absolutely sincere, because it is a question of his salvation, will cause him to bring order into the chaos of his life. These are the only genuine ideas; the ideas of the shipwrecked. All the rest is rhetoric, posturing, farce. He who does not really feel himself lost, is lost without remission; that is to say, he never finds himself, never comes up against his own reality.[14]

In first-world life, it may take some time, but shipwreck will eventually find all of us. It takes time because we have come to a point in human experience where it is possible for some humans to delay a confrontation with their own lostness. Those of us privileged enough to have access to technologies of communication, medicine, and transport and who have the resources to keep ourselves removed from those in real suffering can live for decades without any real experience of shipwreck. But it will not last forever, and when death or heartache or failure finally finds us, we may be so unacquainted with shipwreck that we won't recognize it is a moment of salvation.

When we come to that shipwreck, it will be natural to think that reality has come to an end. But all that has happened is that we have finally come up against reality. Our culture is so infused with ideals—unattainable standards of strength, health, comfort, convenience, attainment—that we will experience a double void: there's not only a problem, there's a problem that there's a problem. A double shame: I'm not adequate, and I'm the only one. I am a failure for having gotten myself into this failure.

The Void

We find an ideal looming over us, telling us how strong we should be, how capable we should be, what answers we should have. What is missing is strangely very present, haunting us with some "superhuman" ideal. Every way we don't measure up to it causes pain, only heightened by how much others seem stronger and more capable. This void of the big things we can't be is an external reality that creates an internal reality—if I'm not able to fill that huge ideal, something must be wrong with me. We feel an aching vacancy, a shameful nakedness in our very selves. We are lost indeed, able to imagine a different, better, stronger self yet stuck in limited minds and bodies, never able to attain that ideal. Instead of experiencing the need for a bridge to cross the void between ourselves and God, caused by our moral failures, we experience a need for a way to fill a gaping void in ourselves—the void between what we are and some perfect ideal we're desperately trying to be. And our culture sees that unattainable ideal and calls it our true self, driving us to try to be it. What if that ideal is something else? Someone Else?[15]

By creating this narrative that our purpose is to avoid suffering and that to experience it is to have failed, our culture has inadvertently shaped a space where God's grace can reveal a void that allows us once more to feel our need for him. It will be a deep relief to discover there is not something uniquely flawed about us when we fail to be God, that he is not ashamed of our limitations. It will be a deep relief to discover that we have simply joined the experience of all humanity. And it will be a deep relief to discover that this aching emptiness was the human reality Jesus stepped into and heals—this is his gift of salvation. Into this moment, the gospel presents real hope. Hold on to that image of the small, limited human, haunted by this looming ideal. Let's take a little time to explore this void we experience and then return to that image.

While this kind of chasm gets little attention in popular, contemporary Christian conversation, it's a common theme in the work of Christian mystics, philosophers, and psychologists. While these writers may vary in their description of this phenomenon, they all acknowledge the crisis that occurs when a human being comes to the end of his or her own power to fix, control, and understand. And they all see immense potential in that crisis.

Mystic and activist Simone Weil knew the very real presence of something absent in the human self. "Enduring the Void is to choose to refrain from exercising power because the Void can be bypassed if one chooses. But it is grace that allows us to face and embrace the Void in ourselves. The energy to bring the Void into conscious existence has to be found . . . because it is the Void which demonstrates that we have need for God."[16] My inability to get us back to Australia invited me into a troubling kind of atheism. My god had let me down. It wasn't until I confronted that god that I discovered it was an idol in my own image. My inability to be God felt, at first, like a deep chasm in myself. But soon that void was no longer shame but invitation.

In their seminal work describing stages of faith, spiritual director Janet Hagberg and New Testament theologian Robert Guelich use the language of a wall to describe this phenomenon. While a wall might seem at first more a presence than an absence, what's absent is our ability to overcome the wall. "[We] are trying to deal with the Wall in the same way we have gotten through life—on the strength of our own will or gifts. We try everything we can to scale it, circumvent it, burrow under it, leap over it, or simply ignore it. But the Wall remains! . . . We have spent our own energy; we have come to the end of our ropes."[17] Since it was my own failed efforts and unanswered prayers that had brought me to the end of my rope, the deep void I perceived was twofold: I couldn't *be* God, and I couldn't *control* God. But there was something better than forcing my preferred outcome; there was an invitation to communion.

Søren Kierkegaard, the father of existentialism, writes with great reverence both for what it means to be human and for all that's outside of human power. The reality that anything could happen at any moment reminds us constantly of our mortality, and it is only by choosing not to avoid the dreadful anguish that we can be led into faith. The abyss of all we can't control is the most real thing there is, and to enter it is, surprisingly, what allows us to float up from the depths "lighter now than all that is oppressive and dreadful in life."[18] Kierkegaard presents us with an oxymoron: in realizing the truth of our condition of creatureliness we can transcend this condition. Even as unpleasant as it is to feel the angst of our human situation, it can actually become a "school" that provides a human with the ultimate education—the final maturity. God had refused to squeeze himself into my tiny imagination, so I finally had to confront the possibility that I was the one who needed to change. When I stopped forcing him to fit my expectations, I could release the angst caused by my efforts at control and my shame at my limitation. Once we grieve the loss of (our imagined) control, a new possibility opens up.

Theologian Richard Rohr has much to offer to Kierkegaard's insights. In his cross-cultural studies of initiation rites Rohr discovered these common themes:

1. Life is hard.
2. You are not that important.
3. Your life is not about you.
4. You are not in control.
5. You are going to die.

I'd felt all these realities in my attempts to shape my own destiny, and I assumed something was uniquely wrong with me. I had to confront something missing in me that felt like death. Although everything in our culture encourages us to avoid empty places, Rohr sees a strange opportunity: "The heart is normally opened through a necessary hole in the soul, what I call a 'sacred wound.'"[19] What a relief to discover God doesn't ask us to avoid these fundamentally human realities that Rohr lists. What a strange and hopeful possibility that what's missing in us might not be shameful but sacred!

Finally, integrating psychology and theology, James Loder uses the language of "void" in one of his four dimensions of the human experience. "[The] void has many faces . . . and all represent the lived 'world' in some imaginative way so as to remove the intrusive threat of nothingness. . . . However we always have difficulty composing out or covering over the nothingness because it is not merely 'out there,' it is embedded in the very heart of the untransformed self. The deepest sense of absence we have is the separateness of the self from its Source."[20] Christian epistemologist Esther Lightcap Meek builds on Loder's language, describing this void as "the deep realization that we might not exist, that we need something, someone, beyond ourselves."[21] There are better and worse responses to our encounter with this void:

> If we deny the threat, or resign ourselves to it, we aren't doing the healing thing with the Void. The healing thing is to admit our need truthfully and cry out for deliverance. This is what happens when we come to the end of ourselves and start to look in hope beyond ourselves for help. We open ourselves to what we cannot manufacture and cannot presume to deserve. We open ourselves to what can only come graciously: the possibility of new being.[22]

"Holiness is not a personal achievement. It's an emptiness you discover in yourself. Instead of resenting it, you accept it and it becomes the free space where the Lord can create anew. . . . Simply hoard nothing of yourself; sweep the house clean."

Brennan Manning, *The Relentless Tenderness of Jesus*

What a beautiful possibility that although I couldn't fix the void, there was a hopeful way forward that didn't require me to fix it! What a wonderful new thought: that the way to avoid the shame of distance from God was to stop trying so hard to *be* God!

Whether they call it a lack, emptiness, abyss, void, chasm, wall, or sacred wound, all these thinkers and many others acknowledge that something is missing. Together they say that human life ultimately drives us at full speed to the end of ourselves—where we can no longer control, fix, endure, or understand. And thankfully, not only do these wise friends present us with the terrifying reality of this abyss, they all find some kind of wonderful possibility hidden in all that's missing. In a culture obsessed with consuming, it will take some time to learn comfort with empty spaces. In a culture ashamed of incompleteness, it will feel raw to confess our need.

Of course, Scripture knows a little something about empty spaces. The scriptural metaphors of purging, purifying, and pruning all speak of something absent. A purged system feels the lack of what it has given up, purified metal remembers its dross, a pruned branch feels its phantom limb. Scripture sees the potential in fasting (an absence of food), solitude (an absence of company), silence (an absence of speech), and Sabbath (an absence of productivity). Jesus's own emptying invites emptying (see Phil. 2:5–7). Even the tomb at the center of our hope is powerful because it has been vacated. While Scripture acknowledges the ache of the emptiness, it also sees great potential in how God can fill it. It is deeply unpleasant to let ourselves confront what's missing, but if it is a place where God reveals himself, what might be possible if we take the risk to feel our not-enoughness?

What a desperate situation we're in! We're tormented by our own humanness, ashamed of things fundamental to our limited human state. Yet this experience of our not-enoughness is

FIELD GUIDE

Which description of the void most resonates with you? How would you describe your experience of the void?

How does your sense of emptiness drive you away from God, to work yourself out of the shame of your own lack? How instead could it be an invitation to depend on God?

simply the human experience. As children we were used to the discomfort of it. We knew we needed something or someone outside of ourselves and were not surprised or ashamed. In the childlikeness of the kingdom, there's a better possibility than our adultish despair. That sense that something's missing is a wound where something used to be, not just a ghost limb but a ghost being, a knotted scar that was once an umbilical cord. Every experience of what's lacking doesn't have to cause our usual knee-jerk reaction of shame, anxiety, and despair. This is just simple recognition that we're designed to be in deep communion with Someone. And if we will be small and unashamed long enough to switch out of our desperate habit of trying to *be* God, we will find a new habit that allows us to be *with* him.

Unsurprised by Incompleteness

Every day presents us with opportunities to experience the end of ourselves—a pain beyond our hearts, a question beyond our minds, a problem beyond our strength. We have a sense of what we should have and what we don't have, what we should be and what we aren't. We experience the lack as pain or shame. And it's easy to believe we're the only one who feels it—everyone else seems to be on top of everything. This leads us to do whatever we can to get rid of that desperate lack in ourselves. We fight to overcome by desperately working to fix problems and people. We work to numb ourselves by doing whatever it takes to avoid our longing and lament. Finally, we just succumb and give in to depression and despair. None of these are life-giving options.

What if the fall is not merely a strange story of naked people eating fruit that, for some reason, they weren't supposed to eat? What if it's also the ongoing story of humans who continue to hunger to be God? Humans who grasp for fruit of the Tree of Knowledge instead of reaching for the Source of All Truth? Since that first garden moment, history is one long story of humans ashamed of our dependence, creating nations, institutions, corporations, systems, doctrines, and brands to fill our aching need for control, certainty, and self-sufficiency. That hunger is the source of every empire habit, every adultish habit. That hunger that could send us to the Father also tempts us to *be* him. What was once a willingness to live unashamed of dependence turns into a way to work for independence. "The desire is for wisdom, for the possibility to transcend one's limitations by gaining new knowledge and insight. . . . [Adam and Eve] . . . decided to mistrust God, to mistrust the word of God, in quest for autonomy that would make them wise."[23]

It is so tempting to do kingdom things in empire ways that even our approach to understanding and explaining the kingdom has been touched by this inclination. This leaves the good news drained of its goodness. Wherever Christians have used the gospel to decide who is in and who is out, whenever the church has been enmeshed with political and economic agendas, we've shaped the gospel in empire ways. Much of our Western understanding of Scripture has been influenced by those tainted readings. However, outside of the mainstream theology of Western Christendom there have been other ways of understanding the gospel, ways that are less driven by empire—for example, interpretations by native[24] and colonized peoples,[25] by women and people on the margins,[26] and by the Orthodox and Anabaptist traditions.[27] We need to invite these other voices again, and not because it's cool or fair. We need them because they bring a fresh perspective to our ways of knowing God.

One significant way of thinking here comes from the writings of the early church fathers (which shape Orthodox theology), specifically how they tell the story of Adam and Eve as children. According to these early thinkers, God's original plan was to shape Adam and Eve to gradually live out his fullness. Irenaeus, Bishop of Lyon in the second century, wrote, "Adam and Eve . . . were naked and were not ashamed, for their thoughts were innocent and childlike, and they had no conception or imagination of the sort that is engendered in the soul by evil. . . . For they were then in their integrity, preserving their natural state."[28] They were able to receive God as God because they were unsurprised that they were incomplete, that they needed something outside of themselves. They were blissfully unashamed to be children. In God they lived and moved without guilt or shame. But they were impatient—childish *and* adultish—and wanted the fullness of God's knowledge before they were ready. In Jesus's words we hear longing for a return to that original state, calling us to become like children so we can live in union again. This childlikeness trains us not only to open the door for the kingdom to enter but also to open ourselves for the King to live in and through our very lives. There is a return to Eden available to us today.

FIELD GUIDE

Does this image of children in perfect union with the Father appeal to you? If not, why do you think that is? If so, what seems to get in the way of living like that?

New (Old) Metaphors

This way of seeing God was salvation! But I didn't have a metaphor for that kind of daily access to salvation. As we saw earlier, Western guilt culture uses legal metaphors. On the other hand, Eastern shame culture has family metaphors. Not "The judge has given you reprieve for your crimes" (an institutional interaction) but "The family has welcomed you in, even with your imperfections" (a relational interaction). In our loneliness and shame, we need family embrace.

Here's where I'd like to share the image from Hebrews 2 that helps me embrace this salvation. But before we turn to Hebrews, let me set up my way of reading it. I'm not implying that the writer of Hebrews necessarily had this image in mind but, on the other hand, it's not an unscriptural metaphor. I've hesitated to use the metaphor; in fact, I've been warned by kind friends that if I use it readers will disregard not only it but also me. But because this image has brought fresh hope to my faith, my childlike courage makes me think it's worth the risk. So I've been praying, trusting again in the childlike instincts, and as I pray I'm also happy to discover that the child in me no longer feels as afraid of the real things my friends fear for me. I'm no longer ashamed of the small, soft, lovely things because I know Jesus isn't. So instead of reacting to that fear my friends and I

"Rather than a pardon or a mercy . . . the gift of the cross is better understood as a new creation. . . . A new people, the God-born, gathered in a new family, the church. . . . This is the divine 'gift' and it is unserved by atonement models that denigrate it, reducing it to tit-for-tat of favors asked and granted and returned."

Thomas Andrew Bennett, *Labor of God: The Agony of the Cross as the Birth of the Church* feel, instead let's talk about the fear before I share the image, in case you feel some of the same hesitations.

The new metaphor for salvation that I'd like to share uses maternal imagery for God. It is not my own gender that makes me use maternal imagery for God. I use it because I'm a child— one who needs both a Father and a Mother. And I use it because I love Scripture, where God was comfortable being revealed in both paternal and maternal imagery. In every way God is not a literal, human father, God is more than a human father. And in every way God is not a literal, human mother, God is more than a human mother.[29] God is the fullness of every parental role—creator, provider, nurturer, protector—regardless of whatever gender categories we assign to them. I sense God longing for us to add to our traditional image of the good but somewhat distant father, the image of the fiercely protective and nurturing mother. If Eastern shame culture longs for family metaphors for salvation, then why not mine every possible positive family connection to understand and share the heart of God? Japanese novelist Shusaku Endo, whose novel *Silence* famously depicted Japanese culture's resistance to Christianity, proposes in a subsequent book that "the Japanese tend to seek in their gods . . . a warm-hearted mother rather than a stern father."[30] Of course, our point here is not to become Japanese but to learn from shame culture to see what it offers. If it's the case that some in shame cultures need maternal metaphors for God, isn't it worth adding a new metaphor from Scripture to our vocabulary for ways to share the gospel? If it's not personally helpful or meaningful to you, perhaps it's worth keeping in mind for someone else.[31]

Apart from any argument I can make defending the orthodoxy of this imagery, there is the very personal, fundamental human need for the unconditional nurturing and intimate welcome of an ideal mother (even if our own mother did not provide it). As Jean Vanier puts it, "We are born into a relationship.

And that relationship that we all lived is a relationship with our mom. We were so small. So weak. So fragile. And we heard the words which are the most important, and maybe the words we need to hear all our life: I love you as you are. You are my beloved son or my beloved daughter. And this is what gives consistency to people. They know they are loved. And that's what they're seeking, maybe for the rest of their lives."[32]

While our Bible and history have many references to the maternal side of God, maternal imagery for God can also be distressing because of how people throughout history have used goddess language—flipping from a world where God was only, literally male to a world where God is only, literally female. If we've read maternal imagery in Scripture and church history (as we've seen above), and we still have hesitation (as I also do), we're left wondering if there are cultural realities at work. Gender has been a political battlefield for at least a century now in the Western world, and we're all a little shell-shocked. My intention here is to be scriptural and trust that stepping into the discomfort of what Scripture actually says might heal our personal and cultural baggage. The fact remains that Scripture uses maternal imagery for God and, at the same time, calls God "he." This is another opportunity for us to remember how to hold paradoxes as naturally as we did when we were children.

"The deeper meaning of the 'return of the prodigal son' is the return to God's womb, the return to the very origins of being, and again echoes Jesus' exhortation to Nicodemus to be reborn from above. . . . The parable of the prodigal son . . . is the first and ever-lasting love of a God who is Father as well as Mother."

Henri Nouwen, *Spiritual Direction: Wisdom for the Long Walk of Faith*

It's a little strange, but I'm comfortable using the male pronoun for God (without imagining God is literally, physically only male) while also imagining the Father is a complete parent we can call "he" (after all, Jesus did) and, at the same time, seeking for the maternal comfort described in Scripture (without imagining God is literally, physically only female). In various places throughout Scripture, God is described in both maternal and paternal language. For example, Deuteronomy 32:18 describes a God who both fathers and gives birth. And Jesus himself was unashamed to compare himself to a mother hen, longing to draw the people of God to him as a hen gathers its chicks. What a beautiful thing that God, when he came to live in a male human body, was willing to compare himself to a mother, willing to confess the intimate care (and even rejection) that a mother feels. This whole conversation highlights our broken, Western, two-dimensional caricatures of what it means to be male or female, father or mother. As we live out our own God-given natures—our protective and nurturing and powerful selves, as men and women—may we become whole again when we discover we're like God, regardless of our gender. And as we all live into the maternal images for God, it may be so uncomfortable that it will force us to confront the negative stereotypes we have of

FIELD GUIDE

What makes you hesitate about maternal imagery for God? What about maternal God imagery do you find meaningful? Even if you don't have a positive image of your own mother to draw on, can you remember a woman in your life who has been a positive maternal presence? What if God is like that?

the generic ideal of "Mother" and the negative experiences we've had with our own mothers, just as we've had to do this work with the generic ideal of "Father" and our experiences of our own fathers.

Having said all that, I'd like to share this metaphor, beginning by returning to the image of a human, floating in empty space, adrift, alone, empty. The human who feels judged by the looming "shame shadow," the sense of something large, revealing both what that human should be and how far it is from that goal. This human creature doesn't measure up—and is empty for it.

What if this large form around us is not a looming shadow? In our desperate state, we've interpreted the situation through our anxiety. What if that sense of some ideal is not an abstract thing but a person with emotions and a will? And what if that person is larger and stronger and fuller but is not looking down on us in scorn? What if that larger being has good intentions toward us? What if that shadow is what we were once connected to? Even the very source of our lives?

God Is (Actually, Literally) the Source of Life

In Jesus's invitation to remain in him as branches remain in a vine, he welcomes us into an intimate connection to him as the source of everything we need, not just for physical life but for spiritual and emotional and existential sustenance. The more we seek independence, the more we also remove ourselves farther and farther from the source of life. If sin is every choice by which (whether by childishness or adultishness) we cut ourselves off from our life source, it only makes sense that sin leads to shriveling!

This brings us back to the maternal image. While we've never literally had the experience of being a branch connected to the vine, we've all had a very real physical connection to a life source through our experience in the womb. We were literally connected to and dependent on another for life. Back then, we weren't ashamed but received it willingly; in fact, it was so much a part of us we weren't even conscious of it. We just existed at one with our mother and had no desire to do otherwise. It's ridiculous and disturbing to imagine that a fetus might even be conscious of its connection or consider disconnecting it. And yet, on a regular basis, adult human beings sever from their own sustenance. We look around ourselves and ask, "Where is God? I'm fine on my own!" and cleave that vital connection, pulsing with life. It's no wonder we feel adrift! We still need daily sustenance that comes from connection to the source of all energy, ideas, and flourishing, but we've detached the cord that once connected us to that source. It's no wonder our imaginations, hope, and resilience have dried up!

If I'm honest, the thought of such dependence makes me a little squeamish. In a world that values individuality and independence, such an image brings up concerns about enmeshment, stereotypes of the overmothered child, the smothering mother, inappropriate intimacy. Where do all these hesitations come from? If the metaphor isn't helpful it's not necessary to use it. At the same time, I've found that awkward places are often places of healing.

Peter Steinke (using Edwin Friedman's work on differentiation) has a helpful description of human connection: "To be separate and to be close are basic needs. . . . But separation is something created for more than isolation. We exist to be distinct from others, not distant from them. . . . We separate in order to unite. We become distinct so that we can connect. Community means two people meet, not two fuzzy people merge."[33] I like to explore this concept by imagining a dozen eggs. If they're all rolling around on a countertop, they have no connection to one another—they are entirely separate, alone and independent. On the other hand, if you took those twelve eggs, broke them into a bowl, and beat them, they would be so close that they would no longer have any separate identities. But there is a third option. If we took the eggs and put them together in a carton, they remain distinct eggs but now are grouped together—a carton of eggs—both separate and close. Some of us like to remain entirely distant and independent in relationships, like hard-shelled eggs, rolling around alone. Others are more comfortable being so enmeshed in a relationship that they lose their own identity, like indistinct eggs beaten together. These relational tendencies affect our relationship with God. For many of us, what he's inviting us into will be very different from our experiences of human relationships. A child in the womb is hidden inside its mother in deep reliance and yet, at the same time, remains a separate entity—each is unique and whole and at the same time intimately connected in mutual blessing.

God as Rescuer Twin: A Reading of Hebrews 2

While it might be strange or uncomfortable to imagine our adult selves still needing umbilical cord kind of sustenance from God, it's a helpful way to rethink salvation imagery. After all, Scripture tells us that we live in God. I can't read Acts 17:28, "For in him we live and move and have our being. . . . We are his offspring," without imagining a child, alive and free in that liquid intimacy of the womb.

Let's return, then, to our image of a fetus. Imagine if somehow a child in the womb could disconnect the cord that sustains its life. Imagine the terror that a pregnant mother would feel to discover that her child had chosen to disconnect from all she offered it. Once it had cut its own cord, what could the mother possibly do to save her beloved child? Here's where the metaphor gets even more surreal. What if somehow she could take the form of another child and enter that womb to make things right? If she could, I know any mother would! Well, thankfully our eternal God has those kinds of creative capacities. When the human Adam/Eve child chose to disconnect from that source of life, God entered God's own womb, taking the form of a child like us, a twin who could relate to the disconnected child. God could be both the one carrying the womb and the one entering the womb. And to be a true help to the Adam/Eve child, the Jesus child had to be just like Adam/Eve.

Hebrews 2 establishes the mission: to bring many sons and daughters to glory. This is not an impersonal mission; we are all of the same family. Jesus calls us brothers and sisters. Since we—God's children, Jesus's siblings—have flesh and blood, brother Jesus also shared fully in our humanity, was made like us, fully human in every way.

Jesus was like us except with one critical difference—he never chose to cut his cord. To be a true help to the Adam/Eve child, the Jesus child needed to still be in connection with the source of life, and he refused every temptation to deny his need for that source. He could offer us life because he still was filled with it. When one scuba diver dives down to rescue another diver who is out of oxygen, they "buddy breathe." The rescue diver shares oxygen with the diver in distress, taking turns breathing from one tank, until they're able to resurface. When this Jesus child enters into the womb, his healthy connection to the source means he still has all he needs for life. And he's willing to make the sacrifice to share his life for the sake of the Adam/Eve child, restoring and reconnecting the Adam/Eve child back to the source of life. Even though the Adam/Eve child has chosen to disconnect from God, if Adam/Eve is willing to connect to the Jesus child, that life force can surge again through Jesus. The Adam/Eve child can be filled with life once again.

Perhaps this talk about umbilical cords is making your stomach turn. Why don't we like to think about this fundamental part of human existence? If anything, we should have a special day to celebrate umbilical cords . . . or at least a deeper gratitude for them! Sure, they don't look pretty but human life depends on them. And here's the thing: umbilical cords don't just carry nourishment to the baby. The umbilical cord allows a two-way flow, bringing "blood rich in oxygen and nutrients from mother to baby" and carrying away "deoxygenated blood and waste products from the baby back to the placenta."[34] And if we're uncomfortable talking about blood—actual, messy, human blood—then we're really not listening much in church on Sunday! Blood is central to our story. Not because we love gore but because blood is human life. Jesus had it and was willing to share it, taking away our "waste products" and exchanging them with his blood, rich in nutrients.

It cost him to do this for us, but at no point in his suffering did he choose independence—instead doggedly remaining connected both to us and the source. Hebrews 2 says that he tasted death for everyone, becoming perfect through his suffering so that he could break the power of death and free us who have all our lives been held in slavery by our fear of death. While we may not often have brushes with physical death, we come to the end of ourselves when we are threatened by existential, emotional, spiritual, relational, and social deaths. Jesus's suffering included all these deaths, and in every one of them he nestled deeper into his source of life. This gave him more life to give to us. And because he clung when he was tempted to disconnect, he is able to help us when we are tempted.

Hebrews 2 goes on to describe what it means for us to receive Jesus as a rescuer twin. Not only does Jesus offer us—his siblings—life, he also offers us a crown. This offering is not so we can rule over others but so we can join him as heirs—with the kind of power that refuses to dominate. He becomes human like us to show us we're glorious like him! He offers a crown to reveal God's glory in us—not a glory that blinds but that warms. We don't like the language of crowns, rule, reign, and kingdom because of how humans have abused such things. But kingdom language is not abusive if we are heirs, sons and daughters of the Good King. God is not that desperate king from *The Little Prince*, seeing every person as a potential subject. Instead, God sees every person as a potential heir to his glory, a bearer of his vitality and creativity. When we're heirs to the King, kingdom language *is* family language.[35]

We feel our human limitations and it brings pain, but we don't always call that a need for God. However, when we learn to see every weakness as one more reminder of our need for God, it's a simple reminder to reconnect with him. Instead of a knee-jerk turn toward independence, it can become a moment to tap once more into the source of all strength and life. So the miracle is possible: ordinary, broken, limited human bodies, hearts, minds, and lives can house the eternal life of the God of all creation! This was what took place when one human called Jesus was unashamed to be human and remained in deep

"This [bold confidence] on our part is the open, unconstrained and childlike approach to the Father, neither ashamed nor fearing shame. We come to him with heads held high, as those who have an innate right to be there and to speak. We may look into the Father's face without fear; we do not have to approach him as if he were an aloof monarch, with downcast eyes and servile gestures, within the confines of strict ceremonial and a prescribed form of address. . . . [Christ] has become our brother and neighbor, and when He invites His fellow humans and introduces them to the Father, it is as playmates, without any formality, or even better, as His brothers and sisters in the flesh."

Hans Urs von Balthasar, *Prayer*

connection with the life source. There no shame or pain or death could overcome him, human though he was.

Because God knew it was hard for us, once we'd fallen from perfect unity with him, to imagine it again, he went beyond words and modeled it for us. We kept feeling afraid of and judged by him in his efforts to engage us, so he found a different way. In our desperate, shame-filled fallen state we could only perceive God as an ideal that looms over our small frames, so God entered into a human body just like ours. That looming sense of what we're lacking, that unattainable ideal of strength and understanding emptied itself so it could be like us. He put himself into two forms to model both his part and ours. God and humans can become one again because Jesus became a human, suffered all the humiliation of limited humanness, and overcame the ultimate mortification, all without breaking communion with the Father. We are in him and he is in us once more. We are whole again, lost and found in him.

What if this void—the ache of what's missing—is because we *are* missing an actual (albeit unseen) connection to an actual Someone? What if the experience of our own human limitation once was a place of natural connection with God? If every sign that we're not complete was once—and can be again—an invitation to let God complete us? What if every sign of "dryness" is a reminder that we're choosing to disconnect from the greening power of God's life? Is it possible that we can rediscover that? Can we set aside the shame of what's lacking, set aside the desperate efforts to be enough in ourselves, and welcome the One who completes us? As we allow God to complete us, we no longer can tell if we're welcoming God into us or we're being welcomed into God. That's the kind of vagueness that childlikeness helps us get used to as we're engaging with God's Spirit. It's all still new to me.

It may take the rest of our lives to overcome the habit of imagining we can be independent. Even in writing this book about connecting to God, every time the task has left me feeling confused, overwhelmed, inadequate, I've spiraled into doubt and anxiety—"Who was I to think I could write this thing?" "Why would anyone want to read what I have to say?" "This is too hard. I can't do it." At times that's made me work anxiously—a working from dryness. At other times it sent me into depression so that I couldn't bring myself to even look at the manuscript. The childish/adultish ways run deep. Thankfully, since the overwhelming work included sentences like "God invites us to partner with him," at some point I was bound to catch on! How freeing it is to remember that every one of those feelings of inadequacy is one more invitation to say, "Oh, that's right! I shouldn't be surprised that I can't do this without you. You're the source of all life, hope, energy, ideas, and flourishing! I need you, Lord!" And while dependence doesn't strike Western adults as good news, it's truly good news to discover we're not alone and it's okay to be human. God is not surprised when we need something more than our own selves, and that is the whole foundation of the gospel.

FIELD GUIDE

What ordinary daily experiences bring up the pain of your need for God? How do you usually respond to them? How could you begin to recognize those moments no longer as a judgment or failure but instead as an invitation to connect to God again?

CHAPTER 8

Rest, Receive, Respond

Christ with me, Christ before me, Christ behind me,
Christ in me, Christ beneath me, Christ above me
Christ on my right, Christ on my left
Christ when I lie down, Christ when I sit down,
    Christ when I arise,
Christ in the heart of every man who thinks of me
Christ in the mouth of every one who speaks of me,
Christ in the eye of every one that sees me,
Christ in every ear that hears me.

—St. Patrick's Breastplate,
Traditional Celtic Prayer

Jesus's teaching on the vine of life helps us remember our umbilical-cord need for God as the source of all life. It's possible to imagine how to rest like that, but how do we also live like that? Unlike branches and babies, we have to get up and do stuff. In addition to resting, we're also called to respond. How are we supposed to parent, work, make decisions, and lead like a branch that's connected to the vine, like a baby in the womb? What does it mean to rely on Jesus's life connection even when we're active and using our agency and gifts? Thankfully, Jesus also has an image for that: the yoke in Matthew 11:28–30.

Just before he welcomes us under his yoke, Jesus thanks the Father that at least the children get it. Even if the wise and learned keep choosing the world's yoke of control and desperation, the Father is pleased to give a knowing smile to the little ones who joyfully nestle under the yoke with Jesus, remembering it's okay to need a little help.

Then Jesus goes on to share his strange invitation. His first words are comfort to tired hearts: "Come to me, all you who are weary and burdened, and I will give you rest" (Matt. 11:28). But without taking a breath Jesus goes on to add: "Take my yoke upon you and learn from me, for I am gentle and humble in heart, and you will find rest for your souls. For my yoke is easy and my burden is light" (vv. 29–30). There must be something remarkable about Jesus's yoke if it's a way to rest! This is Jesus's yoke not only because he offers it but also because he bears it.

It's helpful to compare the world's yoke to Jesus's yoke because we've taken on the world's yoke, even in our salvation. Even in our efforts to take on Jesus's yoke, we're secretly carrying the yoke of the world and just giving it a different name.

The World's Yoke

The world's yoke sets up cycles of despair. It tells us, "Your life is entirely what you make it!" "Fix! Control! Understand!" "Respond! Respond! Respond!" Even as those claiming to live under Jesus's yoke, we shoulder this load and press on, in our work, our relationships, our efforts to survive and succeed, to create an existence and an identity, even in our efforts to please

God. We strive to keep doing Christian things in Western ways, kingdom things in empire ways.

When our efforts under the world's yoke produce positive outcomes, we tend to take the credit and feel affirmed in those habits of self-sufficiency. This perpetuates the cycle. Those with the most education and resources often find themselves in this loop that "works," for a while—we're busy responding to all the questions, problems, and messes, and somehow we're keeping on top of it all. Problem? Respond! Question? Respond! Bosses love this kind of stuff, and it gets us accolades, promotions, more privilege. This is "working" for us, making us imagine we're in control, so why would we try anything else?

On the other hand, that yoke of "Respond! Respond! Respond!" can also lead to unsuccessful outcomes—things we couldn't fix, that we didn't control, that we still don't understand. Our efforts to mask the failure can last only so long before our souls cave in. We tell ourselves, this yoke seems to work for others so there must be something lacking in us. In response we take on more burdens—work harder, read another book, buy a product, obsess about our shortcomings. We're the very broken lamplighter on his sad little planet. And the cycle just perpetuates until it breaks us. Sadly, those without privilege and power very often get stuck in this burden of the world's yoke, wondering what is wrong with them, why their efforts don't get the same outcomes as others get.

Eventually, if we're lucky, this desperate cycle will bring us to a terrible, wonderful moment when we have an opportunity to cry out, "There must be another way!" It is at this moment that Jesus steps in and says, "Come to me, all you who are weary and burdened, and I will give you rest." Jesus's rest provides a different possibility. Although we might think we'd like him to offer us a life of leisure and passivity, free of responsibility, his rest is the partnering kind. His yoke says, "Release control, rest in me. Live in my life, breathe in my spirit, find in me the

187

The World's Yoke

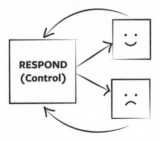

Figure 8.1. What stories of this kind of life come to mind? Unpack the choices you make or you watch others make that represent these different lifestyles.

source of all hope, goodness, courage, and truth. Once you see the things I'm caring about, the things I'm making new, you won't be able to sit still. Join me in my work in the world." Instead of the world's yoke that places on us the demands of a machine (respond, respond, respond), Jesus's yoke has a relational rhythm (rest, receive, respond).

In rest we empty ourselves of our own agendas and our need to control; whatever comes doesn't have to be entirely our making. That setting aside of power does not have to become the power vacuum we'd expect but makes us able to receive a different power, the power of God's Spirit. And from the Spirit we receive an infusion of insight, guidance, comfort, courage—access to strange new ways of seeing, knowing, sensing. Our hearts become attuned to intense urges that our minds would call vague, things that wake us up but make no sense. This Spirit at work in us makes us want to give things we'd rather keep, to go places we'd rather not go, to speak things we'd rather not say, to do things we'd never choose to do. Thankfully that Spirit also gives a joy and a courage that helps us say yes to those prompts. Our resting from our own agendas has made us receptive to the agenda of someone else, and we want to participate. When we're responding under Jesus's yoke, we have not been the initiator of the action, simply the willing participant. If that action leads to pleasant outcomes, we rejoice; our obedience led to good things. We may feel we've experienced God's presence or had some clarity, and it affirms us in this way of living under Jesus's yoke. We continue to rest in him, furthering the pattern of rest, receive, respond.

On the other hand, our resting, receiving, and responding could have unpleasant outcomes. Our obedience may leave us hanging. Our willingness to override every kind of self-preservation may leave us feeling a little bit dead. We assume God has forsaken us—we're only here because he led us here. Why did following him not lead us to more of him but rather to loneliness and confusion? Or maybe it's our fault. Perhaps we misheard or misstepped. While it's certainly worth going back to the Spirit to ask what we can learn from the pain—whether there are new ways we can discern how to hear and respond—at the same time, if we've rested in God and received from his Spirit, there may also be another possibility in the pain. Every prophet was led by obedience to places that felt like death. Jesus died many deaths and then, finally, a literal one. Paul called it carrying around the death of Jesus in his body. If we will recognize it, even when Jesus's yoke leads to suffering, it can be an opportunity to rest even more in Jesus, to find solidarity in his pain, to return once more to the shelter of his yoke. It can be an opportunity to learn how to respond differently next time or to get accustomed to this place beyond self-preservation. Something different is possible here than what can come from happy outcomes. And if we do it right, even this can lead us back to rest in him.[1]

Rest invites us to set aside our adultish independence and remember childlikeness. Here we're able to reconnect to the source on a moment-by-moment basis. In that time when things just hit the fan, that is when we need to rest and reconnect. When we do, life surges in us again. And that life brings with

Jesus's Yoke

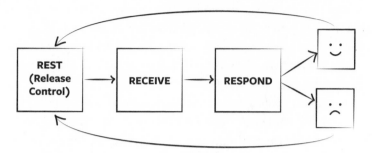

Figure 8.2. What stories of this kind of life come to mind? Unpack the choices you make or you watch others make that represent these different lifestyles.

it a different imagination, an uncanny hope, an otherworldly resilience. It offers a way to respond without fear and desperation, inviting us to avoid our childish "who am I to be used by God?" passivity and take on childlike-adultlike reliance-agency. We become partners, flourishing contributors to the "All Things New" mission, even as we are being made new.

Real, Good News

The gospel is no longer just rehearsing a first-century story of Jesus's life, death, and resurrection or looking ahead to a future heaven with him—although those are part of our story. Now it is good news because it allows us to live with God right now, in these bodies, being like our brother Jesus because we're humans indwelt by the Spirit of the living God.

God has been recorded in closed stories in an old book about a Creator God who made the earth eons ago, a savior God who visited the Middle East two thousand years ago, an eternal God who will call us to heaven someday in the future. Those truths are certainly our story, but if that's all we know of the story it feels like a distant gospel—distant past, distant future. But that Middle Eastern savior God offers a third piece to the story that isn't distant past or future—a Spirit to be with us now, deep communion with God now. This is truly good news in the present.

As we read the Gospels, we envy the followers of Jesus who got to literally walk with him. But that same Spirit who was in him we are promised now, not to walk beside us but to fill us. As we read the Epistles, we look forward to some distant future with God in heaven. But that same Spirit we imagine enjoying in that future paradise he has already given us, not to sit strumming harps with us on a cloud but to *fill* us. We are one with him already. And while we continue to exist in a broken world, groaning to be made new, we see it in new ways when we choose to believe that the brokenness no longer separates us from our Father. When we see the world through the eyes of his Spirit within us, we learn his hungers, his hope as he makes all things new. As Romans assures us, we "who are led by the Spirit of God are the children of God. . . . The Spirit testifies with our spirit that we are God's children. Now if we are children, then we are heirs—heirs of God and co-heirs with Christ, if indeed we share in his sufferings in order that we may also share in his glory" (8:14, 16–17).

I'm choosing to ask, "If I really believed the Spirit of the living God is at home in me, making me a child of God right now, how would I live?" Can we handle the kind of intimacy described in Scripture? Our Western preference for safe distance and individual freedom keeps us from receiving what Jesus is actually offering us, an interdependence that may feel a little too close for comfort.

Christ in Us

It was only in accepting Jesus's offer of intimacy that I was able to embrace good news in that unfinished story of my depression and longing to live in Australia. That story of missing home for eight years became a story of figuring out how to endure that distance for thirty years. And God's good news is active in that ongoing story today.

The good news first became truly vital for me when it got me through a night of intense distress at the end of my last visit home.[2] I'd spent just ten days with my aging parents in the past three years, and I was saying goodbye again. I had no idea when I'd next see them, but whenever that might be, I knew they'd be older and I'd feel even more inadequate to care for them from the other side of the world and even more grieved that I hadn't been there to watch each wrinkle form.

As I brushed my teeth, anticipating the intensity of the farewell in the morning, I reminded the Father, "I wouldn't be in this painful situation if I hadn't followed your Spirit's prompting thirty years ago to pursue education and ministry far from family." As I remembered those long-ago prompts to leave, thirty years of the pain of distance surged through my body. Thirty years of Christmases without family, births and birthdays without family, weddings and funerals without family. Thirty years of too-brief visits and tearful goodbyes. As the pain filled me, a strange mix of toothpaste and tears splashed the bathroom sink. It turns out a whole human body can know heartache. My usual habit in heartaches has been to assume it means disconnection with God. If his presence is comfort then to feel pain must mean he's far from me, that I've somehow displeased him and he's withholding. He's forsaken me. But this time I insisted on the good news that the whole Bible tells—the pain of human existence is not a sign that God has forsaken us!

So I talked to the Son on a distant cross and the Father in a distant heaven. Then that Spirit, which had been the source of those thirty years of promptings, reminded me of our oneness. I chose to believe that the same body that seemed entirely soaked with pain also somehow held God's Spirit. I asked, "How can you be filling me when all I feel filled with is pain?" If the pain and I were one and the Spirit and I were one, then we were in pain together. The Spirit was a sponge that soaked up the pain, not removing it but holding it. Something in me was unafraid; something in me had a deep knowledge of what it is to overcome pain and death. While its power was available to me, I knew it was not my power. In that moment, I had solidarity with the suffering Son and comfort from the Creator Father. These weren't ruminations on a distant past crucifixion or a hope for a heavenly future but a union between my spirit and his, right now, in my body. Somehow that meeting of selves helped me spit and rinse and go to bed, and to rise again in the morning with both my spirit's shakiness and his Spirit's courage. Will we truly open ourselves to Christ in us?

Us in Christ

Thankfully, my children haven't been in many life-threatening situations. But every mother has a powerfully dreadful imagination of all the ways her children might, at this very moment, be in mortal danger. Our gut-level instinct in danger is to hold our children close, out of harm's way. But a mother remembers what it means to hold her child not only with her arms but with her whole self. At times when I've feared the worst for my children, I've felt a deep instinct to draw them back into myself like wrapping their bodies inside my coat to shelter them from the winds—not to smother them but to hold them in that place where nothing can touch them, where they were once safe. It's a strange instinct (especially when I consider how large my children now are and how much this notion would gross them out), and I've heard other mothers voice a similar protective urge.

The more I approach Jesus in my pain, the more I begin to sense this is also his protective urge for his children: not to swallow us up whole but to draw us into himself. When I have invited Jesus into scenes of great pain in my life, I've wanted to imagine him embracing me through the pain. He enters the scene, wraps his arms around me, as my imagination directed, and then he takes over the way I'd written the scene, drawing me not only to himself but also inside of himself. I'm still me and he's still him, and yet we're one. My pain is not removed, but it's held by a heart that knows pain, held in a way that is not afraid of it or overcome by it.

This seems strange until I remember Paul's phrase "in Christ." Sometimes he talks about "faith in Christ" or "salvation in Christ," but I'm interested in the ways Paul uses "in Christ" to say where (and who) we are. This comes up in passages like these: "There is now no condemnation for those who are in Christ Jesus" (Rom. 8:1) and "In Christ we, though many, form one body, and each member belongs to all the others" (Rom. 12:5), and "Your life is now hidden with Christ in God" (Col. 3:3). There's no wondering, no waffling, no hoping we've made it into some grace ledger. There's absolute certainty in where we now have our being. Instead of using the word "Christian," which can sound more like the name of a club, Paul calls us "in Christ." It's simply where we've been placed and who we've been made to be. There are times when Paul seems confused about whether we're in Christ or Christ is in us. Perhaps he interchanges these terms because when we live in this unity it

> "This is the paradox where there is a relationship with God as parent but also the potential for a relationship with God as child, as an infant, for the Christ child to dwell in us."
>
> Fiona Gardner, *The Only Mind Worth Having:*
> *Thomas Merton and the Child Mind*

FIELD GUIDE

If you really believed the Spirit of the living God was at home in you, how would you live, right here, right now? What's the next good thing to do to move toward that kind of life? Even if it makes you hesitate, could it be worth the risk?

becomes a distinction without a difference; we are not just with Jesus but in him, and he's in us.

And he's not only in us as individuals. He calls the church his body, and just as we personally are welcomed into him we are also welcomed into his body, the church, where each of us can be lost and found in community. Together we are him for one another. The actual human body of Jesus carried our pain on an ancient cross, and the ongoing body of Jesus, in the form of a community made of many human bodies, also carries our pain and holds it, unafraid because they know something greater than the pain. We've been baptized into his death, wrapped up in his resurrection. This is how we walk around every day, sharing the same Spirit, hidden in the same Lord.

It's almost as if the Father heard and answered the longing of the Son's final prayers, prayers that also seem to lose track of whether we're in him or he's in us or they're in us or we're in them (John 17). He longs that we may all be one, just as he and the Father are one. As the Father is in the Son, and the Son is in the Father, he prays that we may be in him, and he may be in us. The promise is not only for some future, heavenly place, but in these bodies, these jobs, these traffic jams, these dinner conversations. The promise of the actual Spirit of the living God, existing in human lives, expressed through human words and actions. Human hearts, hidden in the body of Christ, who knows and overcame all death.

You and me in him.
Him in you and me.
Now and forever.
Never to be parted.
Amen.

It has been five years now since that first goose moment. There have been many goose moments since. Each time I've seen geese flying in formation (am I just imagining it, or am I suddenly the center of their flight path?), I've chosen to let it remind me of that initial prompt to fly like that. In whatever way I've been striving to make the world in my image, the geese are a reminder to feel the air on my shoulders and find the sweet spot.

I've been learning those internal wind-discerning skills for five years now, and I've been wrestling with the ways the world around me doesn't always understand where those winds are taking me. It's making me a stronger flier. But now I'm reminded of what it was I actually saw on that first day. I saw a gathering of geese, somehow creating something together. While each goose is navigating its own slipstream sweet spot, the bodies of other geese are helping to create that spot. They're feeling the same wind currents, discerning the same updrafts. To the eyes of an onlooker, they're making something glorious, although they, as individual geese, will never see it.

In all the things the Spirit leads me to do, I'm still eager for outcomes, still anxious for an agenda to be met. Even though it's a good agenda—for the church to be restored to her true calling, for all humanity to know the love of God—it's beyond me. I'm prone to despair when I don't see my tiny efforts creating these vast outcomes. It makes me wonder if I'm imagining what the wind is telling me. The despair makes me beat my wings a little slower, wander off course.

But no one ever told me to make a V. No one ever told me to chart a diagram so I could tell everyone else exactly where to fly! If the Spirit I'm attending to every day truly is the same Spirit we're all attending to, I have to trust that together we're forming something shaped by that Spirit. There will be days when we catch glimpses of what we're creating together. On those days we'll want to call across to one another, "I'm seeing it! It's beautiful!" We'll need to celebrate every bit of unity and truth that together we're finding. This is different from determining what success looks like, orchestrating it, and constantly measuring whether we've yet met our own metrics. Oh, I could design a perfect V. But it would point to me. What I long for even more is for us to take the shape of the Spirit, a shape that draws ordinary people up out of their lonely striving, takes their breath away on ordinary days, and invites them to fly like that.

As we learn these new ways to know God, it will change the way we talk about God. Our dry, old words may no longer be enough to express the ways we're finding him, the ways we're being found. Along with our words, it may take paint and sweat, tears and dancing, to share these discoveries. No longer will we be satisfied to keep a safe distance. We won't be able to talk about God without telling stories of how he met us in our ordinary days and our messy bodies and we lived him.

Resources for Engaging Scripture

Audio Bibles/Devotions

NIVUK (www.biblegateway.com/resources/audio)

Read by David Suchet, this audio Bible is my favorite.

Streetlights Bible podcast (www.streetlightsbible.com)

This podcast is thoughtfully produced to engage global urban culture, primarily youth and young adults.

Pray as You Go (https://pray-as-you-go.org)

A brief daily recording that includes music, prayer, and Bible passages.

Music

Tom Wuest (https://tomwuest.bandcamp.com/album /under-the-shadow)

Sandra McCracken's Psalms (https://sandramccracken
.bandcamp.com/album/psalms)

Yancy (www.youtube.com/watch?v=j1SA744uiCM)

A children's worship leader recorded her "Roots for the Journey"
album to teach her kids Scripture (and adults like it too).

Other Resources

Moravian Daily Texts (https://moravian.org/the-daily
-texts)

The daily texts grew out of an eighteenth-century spiritual renewal of
the Moravian church. Each day they provide an Old and New Testament passage and a prayer. Order the print book, get the app, or sub-
scribe for a daily email.

The Jesus Storybook Bible (www.sallylloyd-jones.com
/books/jesus-storybook-bible)

I've heard from many adults that they've found this meaningful both
for their kids and for themselves. Print, audio book, and video are
available.

Bibliotheca Bible (available for purchase at www.biblio
theca.co)

This Bible is designed for pure reading delight, from the cover to the
paper to the specially designed font. It's free of all chapter and verse
numbers, section headers, and cross references to make reading
smoother and is published in five volumes, each about the size of a
normal book, making it feel like the kind of book you want to curl up
with.

The Infographic Bible: Visualising the Drama of God's Word (available for purchase at www.theinfographic Bible.com)

Rather than an actual Bible, this is a colorful companion to Bible study by Karen Sawrey (2018), presenting all kinds of data in infographic form.

The Bible Beautiful by Alabaster (available for purchase at www.alabasterco.com)

These are books of the Bible printed in a magazine format with beautiful, engaging, minimalist photography.

English Standard Version's Illuminated Bibles

These are published as separate books of the Bible and feature gold ink illustrations and space for art journaling.

The Saint John's Bible (available for purchase at www .SaintJohnsBible.org)

In 1998 Saint John's Abbey and University commissioned renowned calligrapher Donald Jackson to produce a handwritten, hand-illuminated Bible. It is available in various formats.

The Bible Project (Bibleproject.com)

Short, animated videos that make the biblical story accessible to all.

Notes

Introduction

1. James K. A. Smith, *Desiring the Kingdom: Worship, Worldview, and Cultural Formation* (Grand Rapids: Baker Academic, 2009), 127.

2. Brennan Manning, *The Ragamuffin Gospel: Good News for the Bedraggled, Beat-Up, and Burnt Out* (Sisters, OR: Multnomah, 2000), 18–20.

3. Willem H. Vanderburg, ed., *Perspectives on Our Age: Jacques Ellul Speaks on His Life and Work* (Toronto, ON: Anansi Press, 2004), 129.

4. Peter Rollins, *The Divine Magician: The Disappearance of Religion and the Discovery of Faith* (New York: Howard Books, 2015), 163.

5. Jacques Ellul, *The Subversion of Christianity*, trans. Geoffrey W. Bromiley (Grand Rapids: Eerdmans, 1986), 161.

6. I long for both male and female readers to feel seen in my pages. I experimented with avoiding pronouns for God, but it became clunky. I wish God had a pronoun of God's own. See? Clunky. I had tried to avoid male pronouns for God but not because I think God is a woman. The fact is, no one I know who calls God "he" actually believes that God is literally male. Well, perhaps I should say "exclusively male." As James Finley so wonderfully phrases it, "In our own tradition, God is understood as being both infinitely beyond the finite reference points of the masculine or the feminine while at the same time being the infinite ground of the masculine, the infinite ground of the feminine." *Thomas Merton's Path to the Palace of Nowhere: The Essential Guide to the Contemplative Teachings of Thomas Merton* (Audio CD) (Sounds True Recordings, 2002). Jesus talks to and about his "Father." It would be bad theology to say "Jesus" and "God" as a way to avoid using "Father" because of course it would imply Jesus was not also God. As we will see, family metaphors for God are vital to this conversation,

so I'm keeping father language for God while also exploring Scripture's rich maternal language for God.

Additionally, several of the wonderful thinkers I quote also use male language for humanity or their generic subject. Their thoughts are so valuable that I choose to keep their original wording. They lived at a time when this language was the norm (and at least one of them was a monk who lived exclusively with men), so I'll give them that grace. In the end, it's a strange season we're in, where to move away from the old strongholds around gender is often to move into new strongholds around gender, so bear with me as we figure this out one book at a time.

7. Simone Weil, *Gravity and Grace* (New York: Routledge, 2002), 10.

8. José Ortega y Gasset, *The Revolt of the Masses* (New York: Norton, 1993), 157.

9. Anna Carter Florence, *Preaching as Testimony* (Louisville: Westminster John Knox, 2007), 61.

10. Curt Thompson, *The Anatomy of the Soul* (Carol Stream, IL: Tyndale Momentum, 2010).

11. Stanley Hauerwas and L. Gregory Jones, eds., *Why Narrative? Readings in Narrative Theology* (Eugene, OR: Wipf & Stock, 1997), 5.

12. Gary S. Selby, *Not with Wisdom of Words: Nonrational Persuasion in the New Testament* (Grand Rapids: Eerdmans, 2016), ix.

13. Don Browning, *Fundamental Practical Theology* (Minneapolis: Augsburg Fortress, 1996), 6, 8.

Chapter 1: Rest

1. I realize this could all sound like self-indulgence. It's a risk I'm willing to take to help us break our delayed-gratification habits. If you want to use this book as an excuse to ignore the needs of others or the direction of God, sadly, you're misusing this book.

2. Adapted from Katy Smith's presentation at Taylor University's National Student Leader Conference, 2015. Information about Katy Smith as a speaker and educator is available at www.katysmithmn.com. Used with permission.

3. Rollo May, *The Discovery of Being: Writings in Existential Psychology* (New York: Norton, 1983), 62, 65.

4. Pete Scazzero, "Urban Monasticism in the 21st Century" Workshop, CCDA Conference, 2008, http://www.urbanministry.org/f/audio/peter-scaz zero-urban-monasticism-21st-century-ccda-conference-2008-audio.

5. Stuart Brown, *Play: How It Shapes the Brain, Opens the Imagination, and Invigorates the Soul* (New York: Avery, 2009), 59, 64–70. A brief description of the eight play personalities is available at https://blog.zogculture.com /blog/the-8-play-personalities-that-illustrate-how-we-have-fun.

6. Esther Lightcap Meek, *A Little Manual for Knowing* (Eugene, OR: Cascade, 2014), 88.

7. George MacDonald, "The Child in the Midst," *Unspoken Sermons* (London: Routledge and Sons, 1873), 14.

8. Hans Urs von Balthasar, *Unless You Become Like This Child* (San Francisco: Ignatius, 1991), 43–55.

9. Balthasar, *Unless You Become Like This Child*, 49.

10. Balthasar, *Unless You Become Like This Child*, 54.

11. John Collier, ed., *Toddling to the Kingdom: Child Theology at Work in the Church* (London: The Child Theology Movement, 2009), 9.

12. Collier, *Toddling to the Kingdom*, 28, 29.

13. Thomas Merton, *New Seeds of Contemplation* (New York: New Directions, 1961), 296–97.

14. James Finley, *Thomas Merton's Path to the Palace of Nowhere: The Essential Guide to the Contemplative Teachings of Thomas Merton* (Audio CD) (Sounds True Recordings, 2002).

15. Merton, *New Seeds of Contemplation*, 1, 5.

16. G. K. Chesterton, *Orthodoxy* (Chicago: Moody, 2009), 92.

17. Balthasar, *Unless You Become Like This Child*, 43.

Chapter 2: What Gets in the Way of Rest

1. Dallas Willard, *Renovation of the Heart: Putting on the Character of Christ* (Colorado Springs: NavPress, 2012), 122.

2. The stomach is a part of the same neurological system as the brain: "We have 200 million neurons in our gut, which is about the same as a dog (which we consider as very intelligent)." *The Gut: Our Second Brain* (documentary), directed by Cecile Denjean (ARTE France Inserm Scientifilms, Xive TV, 2013).

3. Brené Brown, *The Gifts of Imperfection: Let Go of Who You Think You're Supposed to Be and Embrace Who You Are* (Center City, MI: Hazelden, 2010), 88.

4. This observation from Peterson is from his foreword in John Frame's book *Theology of My Life: A Theological and Apologetic Memoir* (Eugene, OR: Cascade, 2017).

5. Walter Brueggemann, *Finally Comes the Poet: Daring Speech for Proclamation* (Minneapolis: Augsburg Fortress, 1989), 1–2.

6. Joerg Rieger, *Christ and Empire: From Paul to Postcolonial Times* (Minneapolis: Augsburg Fortress, 2007), 2–3.

7. Charles Marsh, Peter Slade, and Sarah Azaransky, eds., *Lived Theology* (Oxford: Oxford University Press, 2017), 11.

8. (Oh, the irony!) Susan R. Holman, "Theology without Footnotes," in Marsh, Slade, and Azaransky, *Lived Theology*, 101.

9. Curt Thompson, *The Anatomy of the Soul* (Carol Stream, IL: Tyndale Momentum, 2010), 262.

10. Sections of this chapter have been adapted from Mandy Smith, "Why Theology Must Take on Flesh and Bone and Breathe into Everyday Life," Missio Alliance, May 28, 2018, https://www.missioalliance.org/why-theology

-must-take-on-flesh-and-bone-and-breathe-into-everyday-life. Used with permission.

11. Rieger, *Christ and Empire*, 9.

12. Richard Rohr, "Inner Authority," Center for Action and Contemplation, January 22, 2017, https://cac.org/inner-authority-2017-01-22/.

13. We are steeped in a history informed by books such as Jeremy Taylor's seventeenth-century treatise *The Rule and Exercises for Holy Living*, where he describes nineteen "Acts or Offices of Humility" and seventeen "Means and Exercises for Obtaining and Increasing in the Grace of Humility." These include: "Believe thyself an unworthy person heartily" and "We must be sure . . . to think ourselves the very worst in every company where we come." Available online at https://archive.org/details/ruleexercisesofh00taylrich. C. S. Lewis describes this as Negative Christianity. See more on this in Gary S. Selby, *Pursuing an Earthy Spirituality: C. S. Lewis and Incarnational Faith* (Downers Grove, IL: IVP Academic, 2019), 54.

14. Michael Casey, *A Guide to Living in the Truth: Saint Benedict's Teaching on Humility* (Liguori, MI: Liguori/Triumph, 2001), 2.

15. Rieger, *Christ and Empire*, 8.

16. For example, Fiona C. Black, ed., *The Recycled Bible: Autobiography, Culture, and the Space Between* (Atlanta: Society of Biblical Literature Semeia Studies, 2006).

17. Stephen Mitchell, *Joseph and the Way of Forgiveness* (New York: St. Martin's Press, 2019), 2.

18. Missio Alliance is a convictional fellowship of Christian institutions, churches, and leaders committed to exploring and engaging faithfulness in God's mission after Christendom. Their resources (videos, blog, webinars, etc.) are available at www.missioalliance.org.

19. Watch videos of presentations and read the outcomes from the day at www.kingdomevangelicals.org.

20. Rieger, *Christ and Empire*, 9.

21. I'm reminded of Wendell Berry's entreaty to "please women more than men" but only "so long as women do not go cheap for power." This is from his poem "Manifesto: The Mad Farmer Liberation Front" in *The Mad Farmer Poems* (New York: Counterpoint, 2008), 13.

22. I enjoy Jane Thibault's language of "aging as a natural monastery." No matter how wealthy or privileged or powerful we may be, we all will confront human realities as we age. See http://www.contemplageing.com/aging-as-a-natural-monastery-by-jane-thibault.

23. I even hear an opportunity to embrace limitation in the repentant laments of Western, white men, grieving their own privilege.

24. Walter Brueggemann, *The Prophetic Imagination* (Minneapolis: Augsburg Fortress, 2001), 65.

25. Brené Brown, *Daring Greatly* (New York: Avery, 2012), 137.

26. Antoine de Saint-Exupéry, *The Little Prince* (New York: Harcourt, 2000). The young prince utters this at numerous locations.

27. C. S. Lewis, *On Stories and Other Essays on Literature* (San Diego: Harcourt, 1982), 34.

28. Fiona Gardner, *The Only Mind Worth Having: Thomas Merton and the Child Mind* (Eugene, OR: Cascade, 2015), 72.

29. James Martin, *Becoming Who You Are: Insights on the True Self from Thomas Merton and Other Saints* (Mahwah, NJ: Paulist Press, 2006), 18–27. Richard Rohr sums up Merton's teaching in the helpful homily "True Self False Self," available online at https://cac.org/podcasts/true-self-false-self -homily-2018-03-19.

30. Adapted to update the language. Isaac Penington, *The Works of Isaac Penington, A Minister of the Gospel in the Society of Friends*, 4th ed. (Philadelphia: n.p., 1863), 2:222.

31. Brueggemann, *Prophetic Imagination*, 78.

Chapter 3: Receive

1. For a body atlas created by Finnish researchers that explores the ways various emotions are felt in our bodies, see Jessica Leber, "An Atlas of the Human Body That Maps Where We Feel Emotions," Fast Company, January 6, 2014, https://www.fastcompany.com/3024327/an-atlas-of-the-human -body-that-maps-where-we-feel-emotions.

2. This statement has been attributed to both Saint Augustine and Dorothy Day. I kept this language even though it's offensive because I want readers to feel my revulsion, not to perpetuate the shaming of women who have been caught up in sex trafficking.

3. This section of text and the poetic description of Ecclesia are adapted from Mandy Smith, "Is the Church a Whore?," Missio Alliance, November 4, 2014, https://www.missioalliance.org/is-the-church-a-whore-2. Used with permission.

4. In my language above of a woman whose heart has never turned from her Beloved, who runs to him at the first chance she has, I want to remember the scriptural metaphor of the church as a bride. At the same time, I hesitate to create an image of a child-bride or an adult woman having to become childlike in order to become a bride. The childlikeness here is something both partners have—the setting aside of safety in order to fully receive one another. Also, any allusion to her purity has no relationship to the abuses of contemporary purity culture; in fact, the church is pure in a way that redeems us all from the power dynamics of that recent cultural phenomenon.

5. To see images and share your own, go to www.facebook.com/ecclesia dances.

6. Portions of the following section are adapted from Mandy Smith, "The Church's Transformative Power Is Molecular," Missio Alliance, March 8, 2017, https://www.missioalliance.org/churchs-transformative-power-molecular. Used with permission.

7. Findings of researcher John Kessler of the University of Rochester are available in the following article: "Bacteria Sucked Up 200,000 Tons of Oil after BP Oil Spill," Live Science, September 12, 2012, https://www.livescience.com/23126-bacteria-sucked-up-200-000-tons-of-oil-after-bp-spill.html.

8. "Bacteria: Life History and Ecology," UC Museum of Paleontology Glossary, https://ucmp.berkeley.edu/bacteria/bacterialh.html.

9. Alan Kreider, *The Patient Ferment of the Early Church: The Improbable Rise of Christianity in the Roman Empire* (Grand Rapids: Baker Academic, 2016), 12.

10. Mark Ellis, "'Fastest-Growing Church' Has No Buildings, No Central Leadership, and Is Mostly Led by Women," *Christian Post*, September 23, 2019, https://www.christianpost.com/amp/fastest-growing-church-has-no-buildings-no-central-leadership-and-is-mostly-led-by-women.html.

Chapter 4: What Doesn't Get in the Way of Receiving

1. Sara Salvadori, *Hildegard von Bingen: A Journey into the Images* (Milano, Italy: Skira, 2019), 147. See also Jeannette Jones, "A Theological Interpretation of *Viriditas* in Hildegard of Bingen and Gregory the Great," Boston University, January 2012, https://www.academia.edu/8271014/_A_Theological_Interpretation_of_Viriditas_in_Hildegard_of_Bingen_and_Gregory_the_Great.

Chapter 5: Respond

1. Portions of the following section are adapted from Mandy Smith, "The Wise Child King," *Christianity Today*, December 22, 2015, https://www.christianitytoday.com/pastors/2015/december-web-exclusive/wise-child-king.html. Used with permission.

2. Portions of the following section are adapted from Mandy Smith, "From Desperation to Revival in One 'Simple' Step," Missio Alliance, July 24, 2015, https://www.missioalliance.org/from-desperation-to-revival-in-one-"simple"-step-the-uncomfortable-but-surprising-way-to-bring-breakthrough. Used with permission.

3. Marva Dawn, *Powers, Weakness and the Tabernacling of God* (Grand Rapids: Eerdmans, 2001), 163.

4. These words come from a blog post that is no longer active.

5. A slightly different version was originally published by the author as "A Memo to Languishing Prophets," Missio Alliance, December 15, 2015, https://www.missioalliance.org/memo-languishing-prophets. Used with permission.

Chapter 6: What Keeps Us from Responding

1. C. S. Lewis, *Surprised by Joy* (San Francisco: HarperCollins, 1955), 86.

2. Eugene Peterson, *Run with the Horses: The Quest for Life at Its Best* (Downers Grove, IL: InterVarsity, 2009), 50.

3. Gary S. Selby, *Pursuing an Earthy Spirituality: C. S. Lewis and Incarnational Faith* (Downers Grove, IL: IVP Academic, 2019), 97.

4. The scenes described in the following section can be found in C. S. Lewis, *Prince Caspian* (New York: HarperCollins, 1979), 101–32.

5. Anna Carter Florence, *Preaching as Testimony* (Louisville: Westminster John Knox, 2007), 157.

6. Jean-Charles Nault, "Acedia: Enemy of Spiritual Joy," *Communio* 31 (Summer 2004): 245–46. Available online at https://archive.secondspring.co .uk/media/NaultFormatFinal.pdf. See also R. J. Snell, *Acedia and Its Discontents: Metaphysical Boredom in an Age of Desire* (Kettering, OH: Angelico Press, 2015).

7. Leonard J. DeLorenzo, "Mary's Freedom: The Hidden Power of the First Disciple," FemCatholic, February 1, 2018, http://www.femcatholic.com /marys-freedom-power-of-the-first-disciple.

8. Rich Mullins, concert at Carpenter's Way Christian Church, Lufkin, Texas, July 19, 1997. A transcript is available at http://www.kidbrothers.net /words/concert-transcripts/lufkin-texas-jul1997-full.html.

9. Portions of the following section are adapted from Mandy Smith, "When Your Calling Feels Like Death," CTPastors, June 2018, https://www.chris tianitytoday.com/pastors/2018/spring-when-church-gets-sidelined/when -your-calling-feels-like-death.html. Used with permission.

10. Barbara Brown Taylor, *An Altar in the World: A Geography of Faith* (New York: HarperOne, 2009), 163–65.

11. Thomas Keating, *The Better Part: Stages of Contemplative Living* (New York: Continuum, 2000), 119.

12. This possibility was first presented to me by Professor Dan Dyke in an Old Testament history class at Cincinnati Christian University. See also Shusaku Endo, *A Life of Jesus* (New York: Paulist Press, 1973), 148–50; and George R. Beasley-Murray, *Word Biblical Commentary: John* (Grand Rapids: Zondervan, 1991), 347–49.

13. Miles Custis, "5 Allusions to Psalm 22 at Christ's Crucifixion," Logos-Talk, April 6, 2012, https://blog.logos.com/2012/04/5-allusions-to-psalm-22 -at-christs-crucifixion.

Chapter 7: A Theology of Childlikeness

1. Timothy Keller, *How to Reach the West Again: Six Essential Elements of a Missionary Encounter* (New York: Redeemer City to City, 2020), iBooks edition.

2. While it has some scriptural foundations, this presentation of the gospel is beginning to be critiqued as Platonic, penal-substitution atonement and is viewed as a Western-linear problem-solving approach. See Derek Vreeland, "Is Penal Substitutionary Atonement Necessary?" Missio Alliance, June 27, 2017, https://www.missioalliance.org/penal-substitutionary-atonement-necessary.

3. David Benner, *Human Being and Becoming: Living the Adventure of Life and Love* (Grand Rapids: Brazos, 2016), 7.

4. Two helpful diagnostic tools to aid in cultural self-awareness are (1) The Culture Test, available at http://honorshame.com/theculturetest, and (2) The Peterson Cultural Style Indicator, available at https://acrosscultures.com/peterson-cultural-style-indicator.

5. Brené Brown, "Listening to Shame," TED Talk, March 2012, https://www.ted.com/talks/brene_brown_listening_to_shame?language=en.

6. Jayson Georges, *The 3D Gospel: Ministry in Guilt, Shame, and Fear Cultures* (n.p.: Timē Press, 2017).

7. Douglas Heck, "Reframing the Gospel for Millennials: A Study in Shame, Identity, and Belonging (master's thesis, George Fox University, 2019), 315, https://digitalcommons.georgefox.edu/dmin/315. Jon Ronson's book *So You've Been Publicly Shamed* (New York: Riverhead Books, 2016) also gives insight on how shame is becoming part of our culture in an online social media world. See also Randolph E. Richards, *Misreading Scripture with Western Eyes: Removing Cultural Blinders to Better Understand the Bible* (Downers Grove, IL: InterVarsity, 2012).

8. Melissa V. Harris-Perry, *Sister Citizen: Shame, Stereotypes, and Black Women in America* (New Haven: Yale University Press, 2011).

9. Richard E. Nisbett, *The Geography of Thought: How Asians and Westerners Think Differently* (New York: Simon & Schuster, 2003), 71.

10. For an example of the gospel using metaphors from Eastern culture, watch the Back to God's Village video at http://honorshame.com/videos.

11. E. P. Sanders, *Paul and Palestinian Judaism* (London: SCM Press, 1996), 75.

12. N. T. Wright, *What Saint Paul Really Said* (Grand Rapids: Eerdmans, 1997), 18–19.

13. Thank you to Ines Velasquez-McBryde for this wonderful language.

14. José Ortega y Gasset, *The Revolt of the Masses* (New York: Norton, 1993), 157.

15. James Choung has created a way to present the gospel that also grows from the ways we feel inadequate. Watch his video at https://www.youtube.com/watch?v=kCVcSiUUMhY. See also James Choung, *True Story: A Gospel Worth Believing In* (Downers Grove, IL: InterVarsity, 2008).

16. David Pollard, *The Continuing Legacy of Simone Weil* (Lanham, MD: Hamilton Books, 2015), 98.

17. Janet Hagberg and Robert Guelich, *The Critical Journey: Stages in the Life of Faith* (Salem, WI: Sheffield Publishing Company, 2004), 114–15.

18. Søren Kierkegaard, *The Concept of Dread*, trans. Walter Lowrie (Princeton: Princeton University Press, 1957), 139–45.

19. Richard Rohr, "Life Is Hard," Center for Action and Contemplation, May 23, 2016, https://cac.org/life-is-hard-2016-05-23. See also Richard Rohr, *Adam's Return: The Five Promises of Male Initiation* (New York: Crossroad, 2004).

20. James E. Loder, *The Transforming Moment*, 2nd ed. (Colorado Springs: Helmers & Howard, 1989), 81.

21. Esther Lightcap Meek, *A Little Manual for Knowing* (Eugene, OR: Cascade, 2014), 35.

22. Meek, *A Little Manual for Knowing*, 35–36.

23. John E. Toews, *The Story of Original Sin* (Eugene, OR: Pickwick, 2013), 6.

24. See Richard Twiss, *Rescuing the Gospel from the Cowboys: A Native American Expression of the Jesus Way* (Downers Grove, IL: InterVarsity, 2015).

25. See Gerald West and Musa Dube, eds., *The Bible in Africa: Transactions, Trajectories, and Trends* (Leiden: Brill, 1998).

26. Mae Elise Cannon and Andrea Smith, eds., *Evangelical Theologies of Liberation and Justice* (Downers Grove, IL: InterVarsity, 2019).

27. To read more about them, see Toews, *The Story of Original Sin*.

28. Johannes Quasten, ed., *St Irenaeus: The Proof of the Apostolic Preaching*, trans. Joseph P. Smith, Ancient Christian Writers (London: Longmans, Green & Co, 1952), 56.

29. This is one of the most memorable quotes from my many classes with Professor Tom Friskney.

30. Shusaku Endo, *A Life of Jesus* (New York: Paulist Press, 1973), 1.

31. Since there are many maternal images for God throughout Scripture, this approach should not be too surprising. See Shiao Chong, "Biblical Maternal Images for God," Junia Project, May 7, 2016, https://juniaproject.com/biblical-maternal-images-for-god. God is a comforting mother bird (Matt. 23:37); a protective mother bear (Hosea 13:8); a human mother crying out in labor (Isa. 42:14), comforting and nursing her child (49:15; 66:13), and never forgetting the intimate, invisible cords that bind a mother to her child for their whole lives. Additionally, Jürgen Moltmann points out, the verbs used of God's action also imply maternal work:

> If the experiences of the Holy Spirit are grasped as being a "rebirth" or a "being born anew," this suggests an image for the Holy Spirit which was quite familiar in the early years of Christianity, especially in Syria, but got lost in the patriarchal empire of Rome: the image of the mother. If believers are "born" of the Holy Spirit, then we have to think of the Spirit as the "mother" of believers, and in this sense as a feminine Spirit. If the Holy Spirit is the Comforter, as the Gospel of John understands the Paraclete to be, then she comforts "as a mother comforts" (cf. John 14.26 with Isa 66.13). (*The Source of Life: The Holy Spirit and the Theology of Life*, trans. Margaret Kohl [Minneapolis: Augsburg Fortress, 1997], 35)

Throughout Christian history important theological figures have used maternal imagery for God, including the twelfth-century Cistercian monks (Bernard of Clairvaux, Aelred of Rievaulx, and Guerric of Igny) and fourteenth-century Julian of Norwich, who acknowledges God can be "truly our mother as he is our father." Fiona Gardner, *The Only Mind Worth Having: Thomas Merton and the Child Mind* (Eugene, OR: Cascade, 2015), 33–34. The Moravian Brethren retained the male features of God while also being comfortable with both male and female metaphorical imagery. Nikolaus Zinzendorf, Moravian Brethren bishop and a major figure in eighteenth-century Protestantism, saw Christ's side-wound as a kind of womb, through which we are all reborn. And Aaron Fogleman points out that Moravian Brethren Bishop August Spangenberg "implied that the motherly qualities reflected the nature of the entire Trinity—including God the 'Father.'" *Jesus Is Female: Moravians and Radical Religion in Early America* (Philadelphia: University of Pennsylvania Press, 2007), 77.

32. Quoted in Conor Friedersdorf, "What It Means to Be Fully Human," *Atlantic*, March 12, 2015, https://www.theatlantic.com/international/archive/2015/03/what-it-means-to-be-fully-human/387550.

33. Peter Steinke, *How Your Church Family Works: Understanding Congregations as Emotional Systems* (Herdon, VA: The Alban Institute, 2006), 31–33.

34. Yuping Wang, *Vascular Biology of the Placenta* (San Rafael, CA: Morgan & Claypool Life Sciences, 2010), 5.

35. For a visual representation of this metaphor in the gospel, see "Good News for Humans" at UnfetteredBook.org/Unfettered.

Chapter 8: Rest, Receive, Respond

1. Note that we will need to constantly guard against impulses to do Jesus's yoke things in worldly yoke ways—resting in him in an effort to manipulate him, being willing to receive from him only according to our own agendas, trying to respond even to his good prompts in ways that try to dominate others.

2. The following reflection has been adapted from Mandy Smith, "The Spirit Is Not Optional: Embracing the Danger and the Comfort of the Third Person of God," Missio Alliance, August 5, 2016, https://www.missioalliance.org/spirit-not-optional-embracing-danger-comfort-third-person-god. Used with permission.